The G in Game

The G in Game

Michael "OoDoo" Smith

Author: Michael "OoDoo" Smith

Cover Design: Pen in the Pen Publishing, LLC

Edited By: Michael Smith and Tiffany Lee

Copyright Michael "OoDoo" Smith 2018 (TXu-2-069-704)

ISBN: 0692051384

ISBN 13: 9780692051382

Words from the Wise
If you want a prosperous future don't dwell on your past!!!

Chapter One

Ooh baaby, yes! Damn you're sucking on my pussy so good, cried out Nicole, who was enjoying every moment of the oral pleasure she was receiving from Miquel, the new mail boy at the law firm she runs. This was actually the first time the two of them had ever met.

Twenty-six year old Miquel Johnson grew up in the heart of the ghetto of Nashville, Tennessee which was and still is infested with drugs and prostitution. He learned about drugs and pimpin at an early age from his dad who had been locked up for the past eleven years. Miquel's mom seemed to have lost her mind when his father left, so Miguel had to learn to look after himself. He was blessed for the hundred dollars a week allowance that his father gave him even though he was locked up.

Miquel graduated from high school and he attended Tennessee State University for a few semesters. Both book and street smarts Miquel was no lame to the games that get played in life. After dropping out of college, he took a job at a General Motors plant in Arlington, Texas where he worked for about five years, but he got laid off. Miquel decided to move back to his hometown of Nashville where he bought a small house in the hood where he grew up. With only four grand left to his name, after he put the down payment on his house, Miquel decided to spend the majority of it on a pound of Gas" (high quality weed). That way he could hustle to keep his bills paid until another job came along.

Miquel landed a job through the unemployment office that he started today. He was somewhat excited to start his new gig this Monday at Smithers & Smithers, a black-owned law firm located near the downtown area of Nashville. Miquel woke up at 5:00 a.m., did a few sets of sit-ups and push-ups to get limbered up before he went and took a shower. After getting dressed in his uniform, he took a good look at himself in the mirror and was satisfied with what he saw. At 6' 2", weighing 200 lbs., dark brown complexion, tattoos and pearly white teeth, Miquel was enough to make any woman melt in his presence. He sprayed himself with a little bit of Dolce & Gabbana Light Blue and headed out the door to go to work.

Miquel clocked in at Smithers & Smithers at 6:30 a.m. His job was simple, to separate all the mail that came into the firm before his "1 o'clock break and upon returning from his break, to deliver the mail he'd separated to the offices in which it belonged to.

While inside the mail room separating mail, Miquel often got interrupted by paralegal or secretaries trying to send mail out or see what mail had come in. Tina, a short, red-boned chick standing 5' 3" weighing 147 lbs., walked into the mail room. She had 46 inches of hair hanging down her back which was accompanied by an ass that you could sit a coke can on top of. Miquel smiled at his mini-scenario in his mind where he was getting behind Tina's ass to do some serious work.

Tina Adams is a twenty-four-year-old from Jackson, Mississippi. She has a body like <u>The Body XXX</u> and a nasty attitude to go with it. Tina came to Nashville a year ago and started dancing at the "Blue Velvet", a strip club located on 2nd Avenue downtown. She was leaving work one night about nine months ago when she got pulled over by the police. The police told her that they smelled weed in the car and they needed to search the vehicle. They ended up finding 3 grams of cocaine in the glove box and took Tina to the Davidson County Jail on drug possession charges. A friend of hers named Charles, whom she had met at her job, bonded her out the following morning. Feeling bad because he sold her the drugs, Charles offered to pay for a lawyer and took her to Smithers & Smithers Law Firm to meet with Mrs. Nicole Smithers, who's known for beating 90% of the drug cases that she represented. However, Nicole wasn't in the office due to a court appearance, so Tina and Charles had to schedule an appointment for the following morning. The next morning Charles was busy hustling and couldn't attend the appointment with Tina, so she went alone.

This must have been Tina's lucky day because when she reached the 4th floor of the firm, Nicole was pacing the floor talking to someone on the phone. She was telling them that she needed a secretary ASAP because her last one had quit without notice for some odd reason. Nicole turned around and saw Tina standing by the elevator looking gorgeous in a tight fitting black business suit. She stopped pacing and asked Tina if she would like a. job.

Being tired of shaking her ass all night long in a strip club like she had been doing since the tender age of seventeen, Tina said "Yes." "That's great! You start now!" Nicole told and went on to show Tina her job duties. Tina has now been working for the firm for the last 8 months and everyone at Smithers & Smithers loves Tina and the two basketballs she dribbles behind her all day at work.

"Is there anything for Mrs. Nicole Smithers this morning?" Tina was standing with her hand on her hip as if she had an attitude.

"No, but if I run across anything I'll be sure to bring it to you." Miquel looked Tina up and down from head to toe.

"Whatever! Just make sure that I get her mail so it doesn't look like I'm not doing my job." Tina said with attitude.

Before Miquel could respond, Tina turned around and walked away. Damn, her fat ass, Miquel thought to himself. Laughing at his own perverted thoughts he was loving his new gig already.

◆ ◆ ◆

Lunchtime arrived but Miquel wasn't hungry so he figured he would get a head start on his mail delivery, since he wasn't familiar with the building, which consisted of 4 floors, 24 offices and meeting rooms. During his deliveries Miquel made small talk; introducing himself to a few employees of the firm.

He stepped off the elevator onto the 4th floor and pulled out the mail for Mrs. Nicole Smithers, but her secretary, Tina, was not at her desk. He heard a noise coming from Mrs. Smither's office, so he took it upon himself to give her the mail personally. The door was cracked open. The moment Miquel peeked inside the office his eyes nearly popped out of his head. He couldn't believe what he was seeing with his own eyes. Tina and some other sexy-ass woman, who appeared to be in her late twenties or early thirties, were fondling under each other's skirts and kissing all over one another with heated passion. Then the damndest thing happened Miguel's phone started vibrating against the door he was leaning on, causing the women to look in his direction. Miquel ran for the elevator, hit the button for the down car, but the elevator didn't open fast enough.

"Mail boy," called Tina. But Miquel acted as if he couldn't hear her by continuing to bob his head as if he were listening to the music playing from the ear buds that were in his ears.

"Mail boy!" Tina shouted louder, but still no answer.

While impatiently waiting for the elevator to open, someone tapped. Miguel's shoulder, which caused him to jump. He turned around and he was facing Tina who was smiling. Damn, I can't get fired on my first at work, he thought as he pulled the ear buds out.

"What's up, Tina! I was gonna come back. I mean, I left the mail. I mean, I didn't see anything." Miquel stuttered.

"Boy, whatever!" Tina had her hand on her hip.

Miquel knew he had been caught meddling around and being nosy.

"Mrs. Smithers would like for you to come into her office." Tina told him.

Miguel's heart dropped to his big toe. He looked at Tina with an "are you sure?" look on his face. Only for Tina to cock her head and point in the direction in which he should start walking. Miquel entered the office with head down like a child going inside the principal's office at school. Tina followed behind him.

"Tina, take your break for the day while I talk to the mail boy for a moment." Mrs. Smithers ordered Tina, who was perfectly ready to stay and be nosy.

"Sure! Do you need me to bring back anything?" asked Tina.

"NO! Just lock the door behind you." Mrs. Smithers replied, making Miquel lift his head up and start to wonder just what did she want with him. She motioned for Miquel to take a seat with a sway of her hand. Miquel took a seat on the opposite side of the desk from her. Tina said he was fine, but, damn, he is far more than her words described. I hope he's not a muscle car with a small engine, thought Mrs. Smithers as she observed Miguel's features.

"So, Miquel, is it?" she asked him.

"Yes Ma'am." Miquel was still acting as if he was in the principal's office.

"Please call me Nicole," Nicole stood from behind her desk and walked around to stand in front of Miquel.

At that statement, Miquel put all his focus on Nicole. My God, she is beautiful, with that caramel brown skin and those full set of lips. Miquel thought to himself. He couldn't help but to take notice that she was wearing her real hair in a ponytail.

She is shaped like a Classic Coke bottle, he thought as he admired her 5'8", 160-pound frame. Miguel's thoughts were turning erotic as he examined her. Nicole leaned down and got face level with Miquel.

"Do you like your job?" she asked him.

Staring into her beautiful hazel brown eyes, Miquel managed to answer her.

"Yes." He answered her while thinking about her 36 double C cup cleavage that was calling his name while they were a mere inch from his lips.

"I don't think you do." Nicole said as she stood erect and walked around back behind her desk. Miquel was lost and didn't know what to say. He was damn near petrified and this woman had him intimidated. I ain't never been shy when it comes to women, so why start? Miquel questioned himself. He knew what the bitch wanted and he was about to give it to her. I don't give a fuck about her husband's office being down the hall. She knows that I saw her and ol' girl damn near ripping each other apart. She got me fucked up. Miquel said to himself. Then he stood up and walked around the desk to Nicole.

"I love my job." He told Nicole looking directly into her eyes. Miquel then fell to his knees and began to push Nicole's skirt upward around her waist while she was sitting in her chair. Then he pulled her closer to him and placed her legs on his shoulders. Next, he pulled her black thong to the side as he got ready to feast on her bald pussy which was shaped like a monkey's mouth. Miquel parted her pussy lips and began slowly licking softly on Nicole's clit.

"Ohh Baaby. Yes. Damn you're sucking on my pussy so good."

He gathered all the saliva from his mouth and applied it to Nicole's pussy, letting the wetness run down into her asshole. Still keeping her pussy lips parted, he rubbed the rim of her asshole with the index finger of his tree hand. Nicole was lost in ecstasy. Miquel started sucking on her clit while he penetrated his finger in and out of her ass. Only one minute passed before

"Nicole was shaking from the orgasm she was having.

"Ummmm, ahh, yess baby, ooh shitt, I, I I'm cumin" cried Nicole as she clawed the arms of the chair she was sitting on.

Miquel immediately stopped and stood up, wiping Nicole's juices from around his mouth. He looked at Nicole with a stare of defeat. She couldn't help but to see the imprint of Miquel's manhood bulging from inside his pants. She wanted to feel him inside of her right then. She was fiending for the dick. Miquel knew he had d her just where he wanted her, fucked up in the head. Um hmm, I got this bitch, Miquel thought to himself. Miquel pivoted on his foot and headed for the door. Nicole called his name, but he never turned around. He left out of the office and shut the door behind him. He heard a "ding" and jumped onto the elevator going back down into the firm's lower floors.

Chapter Two

Nicole Franks married Robert Smithers Jr. close to five years ago, right after she graduated from law school. She was then ready to start her career as a lawyer, but she didn't want to work for Smithers & Smithers, the law firm owned by Robert's father. Therefore, she continued to work as a full-time tutor for the institute she graduated from. Six months after Nicole graduated, Robert's father died of a massive heart attack. The firm was left to Robert Jr. but there was only one problem, Robert Jr. was nothing more than a spoiled brat who knew nothing about running a law firm. Two months after Robert Sr. died, employees of the firm started quitting at a rapid pace, all thanks to the ignorance of Robert Jr.

Nicole thought it would be such a shame if everything Robert's father worked so hard to establish went to waste. So, Nicole took it upon herself to kill two birds with one stone.

She would run Smithers & Smithers to the best of her ability and also create a name for herself as a prominent and competent attorney. By pulling around the clock shifts and recruiting new employees after two years of full-time grinding, Nicole had the firm running like a sewing machine. Even though the firm down sized in employees, it was still running successfully.

Nicole made a name for herself by beating some high-profile cases. On her road to success she lost interest in Robert Jr. along the way. Sad to say, she was never really attracted to Robert. However, during her time of being needy, Robert was consistent with showering her with money and gifts. Plus, Robert seemed to be very sincere at that time when she was in college. Now Robert's lying and cheating was at an all-time high and Nicole was quite tired of it. After all, she was the bread winner of the marriage while he benefitted from a free ride.

◆ ◆ ◆

Nicole glanced at the dashboard of her silver BMW 750 Li and the clock read 3:40 p.m. She took her exit off I-65 going to her and Robert's 2.5-million-dollar home in the Brentwood suburbs of Nashville. All she seemed to be able to do was think about Miquel. Damn, I shouldn't have fucked with him. But his head is to die for! He's what I've been missing in my life, Nicole thought to herself. As she pulled into the garage, Nicole let out a deep sigh from the thought of the misery she was about to tolerate within her own home. She had love for her husband, but she was not anywhere near in love with him.

Robert Smithers Jr., son of one of the most successful black lawyers in Nashville, is a very imparticular person due to his sex addiction. He grew up spoiled rotten by his mother and father. His mother divorced his father when Robert was fourteen and she moved to Jamaica.

She left Robert Jr. with his father and his father to pay her alimony. Robert Jr. graduated high school and attended college just to satisfy his father, but he eventually dropped out. He and Nicole met while he was in college. Nicole turned down Robert and continuously rejected him, but that did not stop him from showering Nicole with gifts and money. He wasn't really interested in Nicole but she was perfect for his plan.

Nicole was about to graduate law school and that's exactly what Robert Jr. needed to impress his father. Nicole would serve as security for Robert Jr. to inherit his father's healthy royalties. Nicole eventually gave in to a relationship with Robert Jr. After they were married Robert then showed Nicole that the only things he cared about were women and sex, while she was left to handle all the hard work and the business. He has fumbled Nicole's heart multiple times throughout the years, but it was about to end is what he didn't know. He stood 5 '6" and weighed about 250 lbs. He was losing weight at a fast pace due to the gastric surgery he had performed on him a couple of months ago. Robert wasn't eye candy but the money Nicole was bringing him home made him handsome.

Nicole entered the house and kicked off her white Gucci heels. She then threw her briefcase on their black leather couch as she walked upstairs to her bedroom where Robert was laying in their California king size bed playing with what seemed to be a dick pump.

"Hi, baby. Robert greeted Nicole in his baritone voice. "Hi Robert," Nicole answered dryly.

"What's wrong baby?" He asked.

"Nothing Robert, I've just had a long day." Nicole lied.

She was really tired of coming home nearly every day to the same bullshit, which was Robert trying to stretch his balls into a dick because that is all his little two-inch dick is. It 1 s a set of balls. Why does he keep trying these pills and gadgets trying to get that little motherfucker to grow? I don't know, Nicole thought to herself in disgust with Robert. He could tell that Nicole was the least bit interested in him or his little toy, so he threw it along the side of the bed.

"Baby, I leave in two hours for the poker tournament in Vegas that I told you about." Robert told Nicole.

"Okay, honey. Be safe." Nicole replied as she finished undressing and climbed under the sheets of the bed to go to sleep.

Robert turned away from Nicole and began texting Brandy, the girl from the escort service in Vegas. Robert's text: I'll be there around "pm, Beautiful! Brandy's text: Okay Big Daddy. I'm waiting. Robert immediately started packing for his flight.

◆ ◆ ◆

Tina sat on her pink leather sofa with her laptop ordering the latest Fendi boots and purse to match, that would be sponsored by Nicole when she received a call from the security desk of the upscale condo she lived at in downtown Nashville.

"Miss Adams, there's a Mr. Charles here to see you," said the clerk.

"You can let him up, please." Tina replied.

Tina arose from the couch wearing nothing but a wife beater. Her half inch nipples stood erect and her ass jiggled in every direction as she walked to open the door. When the door opened, Charles was welcomed in by Tina's body language. He instantly wanted her. Charles was just stopping by to stash something, but how could he not want to fuck Tina's sexy ass?

As soon as Charles stepped in, Tina jumped into his arms. She had always been attracted to Charles who stood 6'0" and weighed 190 pounds, all of it muscle and tattooed like a biker. Tina started kissing him all over like he was the last man on earth. She licked his ears while Charles carried her to the couch. He sat her down roughly on the couch. Tina knew exactly what Charles wanted as well as what she wanted. He stripped out of all of his clothing while Tina lay there squeezing her breasts and rubbing her pussy. Tina positioned herself so she was laying on her back, hanging her head off of the couch. Charles then stood over Tina's head holding his dick and squatted his legs, dipping his freshly shaved balls into Tina's mouth.

"Yeah, bitch. Suck Daddy's balls." Charles ordered Tina knowing how she liked for him to treat her like a little whore. Tina slabbed and sucked away at his nut sack every time he dipped his balls into her mouth. Tina then grabbed Charles' dick and began stroking it, while she continued to rub on her fat clit.

Next she rolled over so she was on her knees facing Charles 1 thick rod. She loved the thickness of his ten-inch dick. Charles took his dick and slapped it across Tina's forehead. "Pow!" Then he slapped it across her face cheek. "Pow!" Next, he entered her warm mouth.

"Eat that dick! Eat daddy's dick!" Charles told Tina as she opened her mouth wider and wider, gripping Charles by the ass, gagging on his dick.

Tina pulled away from his dick to catch her breath. Delirium was written all over her face. Charles sat down on the couch and pulled Tina on top of him. Face to face they clashed tongues. He lifted Tina's body up just enough to enter her soaking wet pussy from beneath her. She had love juices running down her thighs.

"Oh baby, you feel so fucking good to me." Tina cooed as Charles inched all ten inches of his sausage inside her juice box. Tina felt herself about to cum so she bounced on his dick harder and faster. She bounced down hard one last time before she stood up off the dick and squirted cum all over Charles midsection.

Tina sat back down on his dick, shaking and shivering uncontrollably. Charles knew his job was complete so he pumped away at Tina's insides until he felt himself about to nut.

Tina knew the routine so she jumped up when she felt his dick pulsating and took all of his manhood into her mouth.

"Ahh, shit, unhhh, ahhh." Yelped Charles as he came. Tina swallowed every drop of nut his dick released. Afterwards they stared at each other for a second as they shared a psychosexual moment. Tina then got up and went to the bathroom. She came back to Charles with a hot, soapy rag and cleaned his private section thoroughly for him. When she was done, Tina went and got into the shower. Charles got dressed and then put his package in Tina's closet and left.

◆ ◆ ◆

Charles Griffin, A.K.A. Charlie Boi, is from Nashville and he's a well-known D-boy around the city. Charles had a way with the women, especially if they liked "Booger Sugar." Cocaine was his product and any female he had dealings with was either a user, a whore, or their house was a stash spot. Charles started hustling by stealing clothes out of the mall when he was nine. By age eleven he moved up to slinging crack and ever since then he has been knee deep in the game.

He spends most of his nights trapping out of the strip clubs that are throughout Nashville. That's how he met Tina, shaking that fat ass of hers in the "Blue Velvet."

One night Charles entered the Blue Velvet and saw an unfamiliar face which happened to be Tina, a.k.a. "Strawberry." She was on stage clapping her ass which made a sound that was louder than the music playing. Strawberry had all the attention on her and Charles wanted to be a part of the show, so he ordered a thousand singles. He walked to the stage where Tina was dancing and made it rain on her. After he threw the money, he walked off as if what he had done was nothing. When Tina's time on stage was over, she immediately went and found Charles, who was in the VIP section drinking Patron straight out of the bottle. She walked up to him and gave him a hug telling him thanks. They conversed for a couple of minutes getting acquainted with one another.

He asked Tina if she fucked with "Booger Sugar" and she told him "yeah."

They snorted a few lines together and then exchanged numbers and that was the start of their brand-new friendship.

◆ ◆ ◆

Robert's flight landed in Las Vegas at ten thirty at night.

His limo drove him to the Bellagio Hotel where he would be meeting Brandy, whom was already there waiting for him. On the way to the hotel, Robert couldn't help but to think about Nicole and how distant they have grown from one another. He wasn't interested in Nicole anyway. He had what he wanted, which was the money to do as he pleased. Neither did he care if she knew he was cheating because she wasn't trying to be his lover anymore. All she did was work at the firm while he was stuck at home watching porn or playing with his gadgets. Have fun! Robert thought to himself. The thought of calling or texting Nicole to let her know he'd made it never crossed his mind.

Robert knew that he didn't fulfill Nicole's sexual appetite. He also was aware that she occasionally faked orgasms during sex just to make him feel good about himself. If it wasn't for her running the law firm that provided him with an income to do as he pleased, he would have divorced her long ago.

"Fuck Nicole!" Robert said under his breath as he arrived at his hotel. The bellhop escorted Robert to his penthouse suite that only cost him a cool ten grand per night. When he entered the room, Brandy was there waiting for him. Brandy had on a black self-robe that exposed damn near all of her breasts. Robert immediately got excited, totally forgetting to tip the bellhop.

"Ummm, Ummm." The bellhop cleared his throat to get Robert's attention.

"Oh, I'm sorry." Robert said, then pulled out a hundred-dollar bill and handed it to him. The bellhop left the room.

Robert had been anticipating this day for the last three weeks so he was already aroused. Brandy made Robert melt at first sight. He had already paid her a week in advance for their date. She promised Robert that he wouldn't regret spending a dime of the two thousand dollars she charged him. She had him fascinated by the pictures she sent him, but to Robert she was way more beautiful in person. Her half Latino, half white nationality made her gorgeous. She stood 5'0" and weighed a light "0 pounds.

Unlike his wife, Brandy was shorter than Robert with a petite body which made Robert feel more like a man.

"Hello Papi." Said Brandy as she walked towards Robert. "Hello Beautiful." Robert responded while he gawked over Brandy's appearance. He loved her long, silky black hair. "Would you like some champagne?" She asked.

"Yes, baby. If you don't mind."

Brandy poured the two of them glasses of champagne and handed Robert a glass.

"Toast! To a new special someone in your life." She told Robert. They toasted and drank up. Before Robert could bring his glass from his lips, Brandy had her hand grazing over his dick, which was already erect.

"Ooh, Papi. Let Mami suck your dick like you never had before." Brandy squeezed on his crotch not trying to waste any time. Robert liked what he was hearing but there was one little problem. He was shy about his body with new women.

"Oh, um sure baby, but can we turn down the lights and get into bed first?" Robert asked. "Yes, Brandy thought to herself. "That's fine with me, Papi. We can do whatever you like." Answered Brandy, glad of Robert's insecurities.

Robert dimmed the lights down very low until it was damn near dark. He couldn't see Brandy's features anymore, but he had seen enough. Robert sat on the opposite side of the bed from Brandy and got undressed. Then he quickly got under the sheets and covers. Brandy still in her robe, moved closer to Robert then pulled back the sheets and grabbed his dick. She began laying passionate kisses on Robert's lips and placed his hand on her breast which Robert didn't hesitate to massage. Robert kissed down her neck then took one of her firm breasts into his mouth.

"Oh, Papi. You feel so good. Let Mami please you." Said Brandy as she sat up and laid Robert on his back. She then pecked soft kisses from Robert's lips all the way down to his dick. Next she placed Robert 1 s hand on the top of her head and took all of him into her mouth. She put all of his little meat stick into her mouth and jiggled his balls at the same time.

"Yes, baby. Yes." Cried Robert as Brandy took him in and out of her mouth. She treated Robert like he was a charms blow pop. Robert was in another world and loving every second of it.

"Papi" Brandy spoke between slurps.

"Yes, baby, yes." Answered Robert gripping tightly on Brandy's head. Brandy had his toes curled.

"Would you like to fuck me in my ass?" This really got Robert's attention because no woman had ever asked him to perform such actions.

"Yes, baby, I would love that." Robert was happier than a sissy with a bag full of dicks.

"Okay, Papi. But don't hurt me." Said Brandy as she reached over the dresser beside the bed to grab the KY out of the drawer.

Brandy oiled Robert's dick with the KY. Then she turned facing away from him and sat down backwards on Robert, inserting his dick inside the only hole in her body besides her mouth.

Brandy wasn't born with a vagina because she was a man, but Robert didn't know that and he was loving the way Brandy was riding him with his cock in her ass.

After two or three minutes of Brandy's roller coaster ride, Robert was about ready to blow. Brandy heard the change in Robert's morning and figured he was about to cum, so she jumped off of him in a hurry and took his meat into her mouth.

"Ahhh, yesss, ahhh." Grunted Robert as he shot semen into the back of Brandy's throat.

Brandy didn't stop there. She sucked away at Robert's tiny limp, tender dick causing him to jerk and whimper. A few minutes of that treatment, and he couldn't take it anymore, so he pushed Brandy away from him. This is the best it can get, thought Robert. He was in love.

Brandy giggled as she watched Robert trying to catch his breath. She was glad Robert was shy of his body. It was his shyness that helped her to hide the penis tucked and taped in the front of her. She would've hated for Robert to find out she was a tranny before she fucked him. She did great because Robert's mind was blown over this woman he was laying with wrapped in his arms before he fell asleep.

Chapter Three

"Yes, baby. Oooh, right there." Cried Nicole as Miquel drove his entire nine-inch cock inside of her walls while she lay underneath him. With sweat dropping from his chin to Nicole's forehead, Miquel pushed hard and slow inside her love box and Nicole clawed his back with her fingernails.

"I loove youuu Miquelll", Cooed Nicole as she experienced the orgasm of a lifetime. Her breathing was very heavy and her legs were vibrating. She told Miquel that she loved him, but he didn't respond. What's wrong, thought Nicole.

Nicole opened her eyes to realize she was dreaming, but the puddle of wetness between her legs was real. She got out of the bed and went into the bathroom to shower. Nicole thought the hot shower would help her clear her thoughts because all she had been thinking about was Miquel. She hasn't been sexually active lately, besides the making out with Tina. On her stressful days, Nicole would call Tina into her office and they would carry on like two fake lesbians; because neither of the two was real into women. But Nicole had found it more satisfying than what she had at home. Tina on the other hand, had done it for the extra cash and the job security purposes, but during this two month fling, she had created some feelings for Nicole.

About two months ago, Tina walked into Nicole's office and caught Nicole watching porn on her laptop. Things transpired between the two ladies from there. Nicole could never really get into it with Tina because she was from the old school. Some good head and some good dick is what Nicole really desired and needed.

Nicole stepped out of the shower, dried off, and began to lotion up when an idea of how she could get in touch with Miquel this morning popped into her head. She pulled up his job application on her phone from which she was able to retrieve his cell phone number and mailing address. Nicole hurried and got dressed in a Victoria Secret's P.I.N.K. sweat suit with matching panties, bra, and hat. Then she dialed Miguel's phone number, but his phone went straight to voicemail. Damn, thought Nicole and she decided to carry on with Plan B. She got in her new AMG G65 SUV and typed in Miguel's address into the navigational system.

Damn, I'm tripping, Nicole thought to herself as she drove towards her destination. He might have a girlfriend or even be married. What am I thinking about? These were all the thoughts to which Nicole would be finding out answers to very soon.

"Destination to your left." Said the navigational system.

There sat a new Chevy Camaro sitting on twenty-six inch rims and the license plate read 1 PLAYER, so she assumed this was Miguel's home. She pulled in the driveway behind the car and dialed Miquel's cell phone number once again, but she only got the voicemail again as well. Well, here goes nothing, thought Nicole as she got out of the car with her mace in her hand and went to the front door.

◆ ◆ ◆

---RING---   ---DING---   ---DONG---

Miquel jumped out of his sleep from the sound of the doorbell. Who the fuck is this at my front door at five o'clock in the morning? Miquel questioned himself as he cocked the hammer on his nine millimeter pistol while walking to the front door and looking into the peephole. It appeared to be a woman, but it was still too dark for him to really tell.

"Who is it?" Miquel shouted from behind the door.

"It's Nicole." She answered nervously. Huh, thought Miquel. He opened the door to find Nicole standing there and he was very surprised by her presence.

"Hi Miquel."

"Hi, beautiful. Come in. Are you okay?" Miquel stepped aside to let Nicole come into the house.

"Yes, I'm fine." Answered Nicole as she entered the house.

Miquel closed and locked the door once she was inside. He then cut on the lights in his den area. His den was nicely decorated with black leather furniture, a 57" flat screen television and a broad black entertainment system as well. Nicole was lost for words as she looked at Miguel's chocolate muscular body as he stood in front of her holding his pistol, wearing nothing but his boxer briefs. She noticed that he had an early morning hard-on because the head of his dick was hanging out of the bottom of his boxer briefs.

"Did I come at a bad time?" Nicole asked Miquel as she gaped while she stared at his body.

"No, you're good. I live alone."

That was music to Nicole's ears. She threw her hat on the couch and fell to her knees pulling Miquel's briefs down to his ankles then she entered his rock-hard cock into her mouth.

She slowly pulled his cock out to the edge of her lips then locked them around the head of his dick. Teasing and pleasing Miquel at the same time while she massaged• his large nut sack with her other hand. Miquel was astonished. He had to sit his pistol down on the entertainment system before he accidentally shot it off in the house.

Damn, baby. It seems like you missed me." Miquel spoke softly as he enjoyed Nicole's oral services.

"I did, baby." Replied Nicole, never taking her lips off of his dick. She then deep throated his dick down her silky throat, at least as much as she could take.

"Uggh, Uggh." Nicole gagged.

She slowly pulled his dick out of her mouth, drenching his dick with her saliva. Next, she put both of her hands around his dick, placing one hand at the base and the other hand closer to the head. She began twisting and pulling his shaft while she sucked on the head of his dick.

"Hmm, ahhh, shit Nicole!" Miquel moaned as he received the best head ever imagined by any man. Nicole felt Miquel's dick pulsate so she started back deep-throating him.

"Baby, I, I, I, I'm about to." He told Nicole, but she didn't stop, causing Miquel to pour semen on her tonsils. His knees buckled from the intensity of the nut he had busted. Nicole sucked him dry, leaving no evidence. Pleased with her job, Nicole stood up and kissed Miquel on the cheek.

I'll see you at work." She told Miquel as she started walking toward the front door. Miquel stood there wide eyed wanting more of her. One look at how her ass sat up in the sweatpants she was wearing and Miguel's dick started to amp up once again. He took a step toward Nicole, but tripped and fell because his briefs were still "wrapped around his ankles. Nicole laughed at him and left the house through the front door.

◆ ◆ ◆

While Robert lay asleep dreaming about him and Brandy walking and holding hands on a beach of white sand, Brandy was busy snapping pictures. Pictures that are going to change Robert's life forever. Pictures of Brandy holding her dick close to Robert's face.

Pictures of Brandy holding her dick next to Robert's ass. Robert had really fucked up this time and he didn't even know it.

Brandy was feeling kind of guilty about the job she had performed on Robert, but she had already received a healthy cash advance. She was promised fifty thousand dollars by the anonymous source for the pictures that were requested. All Brandy had to do was email the pictures to a specific email account. She pushed the send button. Her job was now finished, so she got dressed and prepared to leave, trying not to make a sound so as not to wake Robert up. However, Robert's phone alarm went off and he awakened to find Brandy fully clothed and about to exit the room.

"Where are you going, beautiful?" Robert asked Brandy as he jumped out the bed, wrapping himself in the sheets.

I'm leaving, but I didn't want to wake you up, Papi." Brandy walked back towards Robert.

Michael "OoDoo" Smith

"Baby, I don't want you to leave just yet. You made me feel like I've never felt before." Robert was sprung. "But Robert, I must go." Brandy insisted.

"Baby, I can pay whatever you want." Pleaded Robert. "I have no clothes." Brandy argued.

"Baby, I will take you shopping. Just come here and let Big Daddy take good care of you."

"Robert, I must leave to get myself together, but I can return at noon if that's okay with you." Brandy lied.

Robert stood there watching Brandy and he could see that some thing was wrong with her. He didn't want to be the reason that Brandy may get in any trouble with the escort service, so he agreed to her offer.

"Baby, pinky promise me that you will return to me by noon and I promise you that we can go shopping or whatever you want to do. I just want you in my presence." Robert told Brandy, being more serious than a heart attack with her.

Brandy's heart sank into her big toe as she listened to the nicest words any man had ever spoken to her. She couldn't hold back her emotions and a tear leaked from her eye. Before she knew it, she had tightly embraced Robert.

"Baby, it's gonna be okay. Big Daddy promises you that."

Robert meant every single word of that. How could someone hurt someone as beautiful and special as Brandy?" Robert thought to himself.

Brandy released her hold on Robert. She pinky promised him that she would return by noon and gave him a kiss on the lips. Robert felt electricity flow through his body from her kiss.

Robert immediately started planning an exclusive evening to delight Brandy with.

Brandy was born Brandon Santos. His mother, Vanessa, was Latin and his father was White. Brandon never knew his father because his mother had gotten pregnant while she was working the prostitution track in Las Vegas. Brandon grew up playing with baby dolls, wearing make-up,

20

and dressing like a girl. His mom thought it was cute, plus she always wanted a little girl.

One night when Brandon was ten years old, Vanessa was out working and her boyfriend came home drunk. He caught Brandon fully dressed like a woman.

"Come here you little punk muthafucka." He demanded of Brandon right before he slapped blood from Brandon's mouth.

"So you wanna be a bitch? Huh boy? Boy you betta answer me." The man yelled, but Brandon remained silent. The man threw Brandon onto the bed face down and held him down by the neck. Brandon started crying and weeping as he heard the man unbuckling his belt.

"Since you wanna be a bitch, how does this feel?" The enraged man growled into Brandon's ear as he forced his manhood into little Brandon's tiny butt hole.

Brandon just laid there crying and took the man inside of him. Somewhere deep down inside Brandon, he was enjoying this experience even though it hurt so bad. That's the night that Brandy was born.

Brandy sat in the back of the cab with tears flowing from her eyes like a river. She felt so bad for scandalizing Robert. She may have just betrayed the one man who might have loved her for who she was. Brandy felt as if Robert might accept her if she poured out her soul and let Robert know that she was a man. She felt so stupid. She wasn't even from an escort service. The escort service was made up by Brandy on a rake page that she used to make money off of. Three weeks ago when she received a phone call from Robert, she had no idea that he would be so intrigued by her. Most men knew at first sight that Brandy was a man. Some carried on with sexual pleasure, some men beat up Brandy, and some scared the hell out of her. Hell, she even got pistol whipped by one guy who realized that she had an Adam's apple.

Brandy had been through so much in life and now she finally had the money she needed for her sex change. All thanks to the person who so badly wanted Robert framed. A week before today she received a phone call from an unidentified woman offering $50,000 for Brandy to take pictures of her performing hideous sexual acts with Robert. Then Brandy was to email the pictures to the woman. The $50,000 would be deposited in Brandy's account as soon as the pictures were received by the person who wanted them. Knowing she had held down her part of the deal, Brandy logged on the bank's app with her phone to check her account.

Sure enough, $50,000 had been deposited into her account. Brandy cried even harder.

◆ ◆ ◆

Miquel managed to make it to work on time this morning. He listened to his iPod while he separated the mail, but his thoughts were somewhere else. I'm not about to allow Nicole to play with my feelings and emotions, nor will she be able to play with my intelligence. I'm a player, but this bitch got me wanting to hang my jersey up and I don't even know her, thought Miquel. It was something about Nicole that made him weak for her. He wanted to go to the 4th floor and barge into her office so bad, but he fought the urge with all his might. He refused to open up to Nicole just for her to shoot him down. Coming out of his thoughts, he looked up to find Tina standing in the doorway looking like she had something on her mind.

Tina's fine thick ass stood in the door wearing a black and white checkered mini-skirt with a white blouse that her breasts were about to jump out of.

"What's up, Ma! Can I help you with something?" Miquel asked Tina. But there was no response. Tina closed the door and walked towards Miquel reaching for his crotch, but he declined the offer. By him saying no to her, it only made Tina throw herself at him even more.

"Chill out, Ma! What's up with you?" Miquel moved her hands away from him and stepped out of her reach.

"Stop frontin' like you don't want me Miquel. You know you do." Tina told Miquel while she tried to seduce him.

"Tina, straight up Ma, I'm not interested." Miquel stated firmly and Tina immediately stopped trying.

"Smile for the camera Miquel." Tina pointed to the surveillance camera on the wall. Tina burst into laughter and walked out of the mailroom. Miquel had already known what was going on from the get go. Why settle for bologna sandwich when he has a steak dinner waiting for him, thought Miquel. He looked up at the surveillance camera and stuck up his middle finger, then went back to work.

◆　◆　◆

As Nicole watched the monitor it was as if her heart had stopped umping until she saw Miquel rejecting Tina.

"Shoo!" Exhaled Nicole. What a relief, she thought. Now Nicole was at her desk laughing at Miquel as he flicked off the camera.

"Looks like he's a winner, Boss Lady." Said Tina as she entered Nicole's office.

"Yeah, I know, huh! Hell, I couldn't even turn down that fat ass of yours." Said Nicole and then the two of them burst into laughter.

"Well, I guess that's it for us, huh?" Said Tina, trying not to sound mad that Nicole had fallen for Miquel.

"Tina, you know damn well neither of us really likes women." Exclaimed Nicole as she stood from her seat.

"I know, right." Tina replied and they laughed again. "So what are your plans with Miquel, .Boss Lady?"

"I don't want to rush anything. He may not be ready for what I'm wanting to do. "Nicole said through stretching her arms in the air.

"I feel that." Replied Tina.

"Oh, so you do." Nicole walked to lock the door and then creeped up behind Tina and licked Tina's neck with her tongue, causing Tina to squirm in her chair.

"Yes, I doooo!!" Cooed Tina while reaching back and grabbing Nicole's head as Nicole nibbled on her ear.

"That's still my pussy, isn't it?" Whispered Nicole as she rubbed between Tina's thighs.

"Yessss Bossss Laddyyyy." Answered Tina as she felt her love box moisten. She opened her thighs for Nicole to explore.

Nicole rubbed further up Tina's thighs finding her clit and began rubbing on it in a circular motion causing Tina's pussy to get wetter and wetter. For some reason this intimate session between Nicole and Tina felt more natural between the two of them than ever before. They both realized it as they took each other's tongues into one another's mouth. Erogenous feelings occurred.

This time feels real, thought Nicole as she extracted her hand away from Tina's vagina.

"That's enough!" Proclaimed Tina as she stood up fixing her skirt. She was feeling some type of way.

"I agree." Nicole replied and walked around to sit at her desk as Tina walked out of the office."

Chapter Four

Miquel clocked out for his lunch break at 11:00 a.m. and walked to the parking garage where his car was parked. When he reached his car, he noticed that a note had been stuck under his windshield wiper.

"Meet me at Ruth Chris Baby!!" Read the note.

Fifteen minutes later, he was arriving at Ruth Chris Steak house where a valet parked his car for him. Miquel entered the steakhouse and the hostess led him to a table where Nicole was waiting for him. He walked to Nicole, hugged her around her neck, and kissed her on the cheek. Nicole noticed Miquel 1 s actions towards her were bolder than the previous day when they first met. He seemed to be totally comfortable with her and that made Nicole feel pretty good.

"What are we eating, baby'? I'm hungry as fuck." Stated Miquel.

"I ordered us both T-bones well done, gumbo, baked potatoes, and salads." Nicole answered smiling at Miquel.

"That sounds good, but let 1 s cut past the bullshit. What are your plans with me, beautiful? "Asked Miquel catching Nicole off guard with his question, as he grabbed a piece of baked bread from the basket on the table.

"What do you mean, handsome?" Asked Nicole as if she didn't understand what Miquel was talking about.

"You know exactly what I mean! What, you think I'm gonna accept whatever position you have got planned for me in Miss Nicole's world?" Miquel asked her as he bit into his buttered bread.

"Miquel, I don't... Nicole started to say before Miquel cut her off.

"Look, Nicole, I'm not a fucking child so don't play any silly ass games with me. I know you're married as well as I know that you and Tina are fucking. So I'm going to ask you one more fucking time. What are you planning on doing with me?" Miquel said firmly to Nicole as he chewed on his bread.

Nicole had been caught off guard by Miquel's sudden mood change. The aggressiveness of his voice and the seriousness, in his eyes confirmed that he wasn't playing any games. I wasn't ready for this, thought Nicole. She was used to being the one in control. Nicole didn't know what to say, but before she could say anything, Miquel started speaking again.

"And the next time you decide to pop up at my house, make sure you bring Tina with you so I can fuck both of ya'll.

Since you wanna play these immature lil girl ass games, I'm gonna treat you like a little ass girl." Miquel told Nicole then took a sip of his water.

"Oh, yeah. I need some money, babe. My fucking bills are behind." Miquel added.

Nicole had never been talked to in such a manner, but it felt good to her to be sitting beside a man who wasn't afraid of her. He wasn't afraid to tell her how he felt, nor was he afraid to tell her what he wanted. Nicole instantly fell in love with Miquel right then and there. She began to tear up as she looked into Miguel's eyes, then she began to talk.

"You can have whatever you want, Miquel, as long as I can have you. I truly believe we will make each other happy. Let me get things squared away with my husband so you and I can go on with our lives as one. Can you give me some time to handle my situation with my marriage?" Nicole spoke with her heart, wanting Miquel to feel and understand where she was coming from.

"I can do that, baby." Miquel told Nicole. Then he leaned over and kissed her on the lips.

"Where the fuck is our food at?" Miquel said out loud right after he kissed Nicole.

"Here you are, sir!" Responded the server who happened to hear Miquel. Nicole and Miquel burst into laughter.

Miquel and Nicole enjoyed their lunch as they got acquainted with one another, and filled one another in on their current situations. They found out that they shared common interests in food, movies, and much more. The two were having a great time until Tina walked towards them throwing cards, teddy bears, dead roses, and other objects at their table. Nicole couldn't believe what was happening. Tina was very irate and crying all the while yelling obscenities towards Nicole.

"How dare you play with my heart, Nicole? I HATE you BITCH!" Screamed Tina through her tears. Miquel sat there amused at the show he was watching.

"Ma'am, you have to leave." Said the security officer while grabbing Tina and carrying her out of the restaurant.

"Get your fucking hands off me! All you bitches gonna die!" Yelled Tina as she got carried out of the restaurant.

"Damn, baby. I knew ya'll were fucking around, but it seems ya'll were fucking around the long way." Miquel said, laughing as he pulled a vibrator from out of his gumbo soup.

Nicole was so embarrassed. What the fuck just happened? Thought Nicole as the alarms went off on both of their keypads to their cars. They got up from the table and walked to the parking garage to find bricks thrown through both of their windshields.

DAMN! This bitch is possessed, thought Nicole, as she examined her car. She then took out her checkbook and wrote Miquel a check for $3,000.

"Here, baby. Take the rest of the day off and I'll catch up with you later. "Nicole told Miquel as she handed him the check".

"Thanks, baby!" Miquel kissed Nicole on the lips.

They both got inside their cars to depart. Miquel rolled down his window and blew the horn in order to get Nicole's attention. She rolled down her window when she heard the horn.

"Yes, Hunny!" Asked Nicole.

"Get your bitch under control." Miquel said playfully.

"Arrggghhh Miquel ...." Was all Nicole got out of her mouth before "Schrruum" Miquel peeled rubber out of the parking garage.

Tina drove to her home in an uproar, speeding down the highway in her new baby blue Lexus 460. She cried alligator tears while listening to Dru Hill's "Somebody's sleeping in my bed" on the stereo. How dare Nicole play with my feelings like this, Tina asked herself as if she and Nicole were in a committed relationship. Bitch buying the gifts and shit. Telling me she loves me, just to toss me to the side for the fucking mail boy, thought Tina as she took her exit going home.

Once she got inside her home, Tina felt she needed to escape the pain that she was enduring. She went to her room closet and found Charles' stash of cocaine that he hides at her home. She opened the shoe box and found inside 36 separate sandwich bags, each filled with an ounce of cocaine. She grabbed one of the bags and put the rest back in the closet. Tina grabbed a plate from the kitchen and went and sat on her couch. She poured the cocaine onto the plate.

Next, she grabbed a dollar bill from her purse and rolled it up. "Sniff, Sniff." Tina's face immediately went numb as she laid back on the couch listening to the sound of her heart beating. She was now feeling palatial as the coke pacified her emotions. How am I gonna repay this bitch for the way she handled me, Tina asked herself, thinking about her revenge against Nicole.

"Bitch, you know how to get that bitch back for what she did to you." The cocaine said to Tina.

Tina began looking around the room like there was someone in there with her besides the cocaine. Seeing there wasn't another soul there with her, she looked at the plate of cocaine.

"How is that?" Tina asked the cocaine.

"Sniff a couple more lines and I'll tell you how." The cocaine told her.

"Okay!" Tina replied. Then she broke down two lines of cocaine and snorted them.

"Good girl! Robert, Robert, Robert!" Shouted the cocaine. Tina laid back on the couch, smiling and laughing at her own perverse thoughts that were rolling through her mind.

◆ ◆ ◆

It was now 1 o'clock p.m. and Robert still hadn't heard from Brandy. He called her phone several times, only managing to get her voicemail. He left multiple messages before he decided that he could take the first flight back to Nashville. Before booking his flight, Robert decided that he had to call Nicole.

"Hello." Nicole answered the phone.

"Hi, gorgeous."

"Hi, Robert." Nicole spoke dryly. "What are you doing?"

"I'm on the phone with a client right now, so I need to call you back if it's not urgent." Nicole told Robert.

"Oh, okay. Handle your business. I'm about to book me a flight for this evening. I got eliminated from the tournament this morning, so I should be back around eleven tonight." Robert told Nicole.

"Okay, Robert. I'll see you when you return." Nicole hung up on Robert.

Stinky bitch, thought Robert as he heard the phone hung up.

Robert was fed up with women treating him like he wasn't the king and decided he would show his power once he returned to Nashville. I'm gonna show these bitches once and for all who Robert Smithers Jr. is, Robert thought to himself as he called the airport to book his flight.

♦ ♦ ♦

Nicole returned to work and called on the windshield service whom told her they'll be there in thirty minutes to repair her windshield. After hanging up the phone, she sat at her desk thinking about the series of events that had taken place in the last 36 hours. Out of the events, the only thing, she was pleased with was Miquel. Was I wrong for leading Tina on? Thought Nicole.

No, she answered herself. Tina should have known how to control her feelings and emotions, just like I do, thought Nicole.

Nicole was tired of running the law firm only to let Robert run around living life like a rich bachelor. She was unhappy, but Nicole had a plan to change all of that very soon. She sat in disgust as she looked at the pictures she had received from a transsexual in Las Vegas that Robert had fucked. Nicole couldn't help but laugh at Robert on the pictures being the stupid mother fucker he was, laying in the bed, sound asleep with a dick inches away from his lips. He must know that he'll never get this pretty pussy again, Nicole thought to herself. She was glad that she finally held in her possession what it would take to get Robert out of her life forever. $50,000 well spent, thought Nicole, the best payment ever.

Two weeks ago, Nicole made it home early to find Robert sleeping like a baby on the couch. She tried to wake him up, but he seemed to be drained because he continued to snore and didn't move. Nicole noticed his phone was blowing up with messages, so she picked it up and went upstairs into the bathroom, locking the door behind her. When she unlocked Robert's phone, Nicole couldn't believe how reckless he'd become about leaving evidence to all his messages in his phone.

One particular message caught Nicole's attention. Who is this Brandy bitch from Vegas Escorts, who just texted him talking about she can't wait to see Papi in two weeks? Nicole, asked herself. She immediately went into investigator mode and after three days of investigating, Nicole found Brandy out and discovered that she really was Brandon and running a fake escort service. She even talked to Brandy and offered her $50,000 for some humiliating pictures of Brandy and Robert when he came to Vegas. Brandy swore she couldn't wait to deliver the pictures in exchange for the cash. To seal the deal, Nicole sent Brandy $5,000 that day. Nicole couldn't wait to see if Robert was dumb enough to go to Vegas and have sex with a chump. Just as she thought ... he was. Mission accomplished! Nicole snapped out of her thoughts when the next message alert went off on her phone. It was from Miquel. "On ah nigga mind." Read the message. Nicole couldn't help but smile as she melted like butter on hot toast.

"Same here chocolate drop." Replied Nicole. She waited for Miquel to text her back but he didn't. This man has me gone, thought Nicole.

◆ ◆ ◆

Miquel had just left the bank after cashing the check from Nicole when he received the text from her. "Chocolate Drop" thought Miquel as he pulled into the Chevy dealership to get his windshield fixed. The dealership told Miquel it would be a day before they could fix it and gave him a loaner car.

Leaving the dealership riding low key in a new Chevy Impala, Miquel started thinking about how Nicole could be everything he needed and more. I could stop nickel and liming in the hood selling weed and open up some type of business. I want a car lot, thought Miquel. When he pulled into his driveway he got a call from a classmate, Charles, who wanted to come by and grab something to smoke. He told Charles to come on through. Miquel went inside his house and gathered his entire stock that he had left. He decided that he was done peddling in the drug game.

Besides, his dad was going up for parole next month and would need somewhere safe to parole out to. Charles knocked at the door.

"Come in!" Yelled Miquel.

"What's up, my nigga. You riding that new thang ain't ya?" Said Charles as he walked through the door.

"Nah G. It's a loaner. What's good though?" "Shit. Been chillin. You know me."

"I feel that. They got my clocking in again."

"I see ya uniform nigga. One of my lil bitches work down there."

"Who is she?" I ain't trying to step on no toes." Miquel said, laughing as he searched for his digital scale.

"Ah, lit red bitch named Tina. She used to work at the "Blue Velvet" till she caught a lit possession case leaving work." Charles explained.

"Righteous." Responded Miquel. This is a small world, Miquel thought.

"That hoe a squirter too, nigga. So you might wanna get some of that pussy, but I must warn you, the bitch is a nympho. She can go all night, especially if she on dat "Booger Sugar". Charles said with plenty of sarcasm.

Miquel acted as if he wasn't paying attention to Charles, but he was indeed. This explains everything, thought Miquel.

"She been working there about seven or eight months now." Said Charles, continuing to run off at the mouth as he pulled out a quarter bag of cocaine.

"Do you mind, my nigga?" Charles asked Miquel, not wanting to disrespect him.

"Nah. Go ahead my nigga!" Miquel replied as he bagged the weed.

"Sniff, Sniff!" "Yeah, I think her and that fine ass lawyer she work for got something going but that bitch Tina won't let a nigga in." Charles continued to babble off as he cleaned his nose and put the rest of the coke back in his pocket.

"What you had wanted?"

"Give me something for one-fifty." Charles told Miquel as he handed him the money.

"Here, bruh. Take all this shit. I'm through fucking around."

Miquel gave Charles all the weed he had which was triple the amount, Charles paid for.

"Damn, nigga! That's what's up! You must've hit the lotto nigga." Charles said, laughing.

"Nah, bruh. Just shutting down shop. Pops comin home."

"I see," Said Charles.

"Yeah. He comes home next month. So I'm gonna give this shit up! Don't wanna have shit here when he gets out. Know what I'm talking about?" Miquel explained.

"Hell yeah! Hell yeah, my G." Answered Charles as he prepared to leave.

They gave each other daps and Charles left. Miquel sat on the couch, astonished by everything he had heard from Charles. Man, this shit is heavy, thought Miquel. Did Nicole fuck around with cocaine? Is that why that bitch came up in the restaurant like that? Fuck all this shit! Ain't got time to try to figure it out. All I know is I gotta do what's best for me. Thought Miquel, and he started singing. Gucci Mane's song "Back On" as he walked to his room to get prepared for the night.

Chapter Five

Hours had passed since Brandy ignored Robert's phone calls. When she left the hotel, Brandy was so confused she didn't know what to do, so she decided to go shopping. Brandy was feeling like a real diva as she walked through the Galleria holding more bags than she could carry in her arms. The hell with a sex change!

A lot of my clients like the tool I possess between my legs and maybe Robert would also if I exposed myself to him, thought Brandy as she walked out of the Galleria with her mind racing nonstop.

Brandy left the Galleria and went to an Asian saloon where she was a regular customer. When she entered the saloon, it was empty except where she was a regular customer. When she entered the saloon it was empty except for Henry, who's real name was Tran Thao. Most of the Asian men Brandy knew were bisexuals, but their wives didn't know. Neither did their wives know that they smoked crack as a recreational drug as well.

"Hi, Henry. Where's your wife? I need to get my body waxed."

Said Brandy, sexy. "She leave. Maybe I can help you. "Said Henry, who was glad to see Brandy.

"Sure. Why not?" Said Brandy as she sat in a massage chair.

Henry darted to the back of the shop and came back blowing out smoke as he walked to the front door and locked it.

"Henry, you closing?" Asked Brandy.

"No more customer. Me smoka crack." Said Henry.

Brandy burst into laughter as she watched Henry walk back to the back of the shop. He stayed in the back way too long for Brandy's patience.

"Henry!" Brandy yelled.

"Come bak hure. Come bak hure." Henry yelled back to Brandy.

Brandy, knowing what Henry wanted, walked to the back of the shop where Henry was, in a small room where the supplies were kept. Henry was butt naked holding a crack pipe.

"Fuck me, fuck me in my ass! I pay you good!" Said Henry as he bent over and held onto the shelf mounted against the wall.

Brandy pulled her skin tight jeans down around her ankles and un-taped her cock. She began stroking her cock to get an erection going, which was sometimes challenging due to her manhood being tucked away so much. By the time she got an erection going, the alarm to the salon went off.

---BACK DOOR OPEN--- Sounded the alarm.

"Sie hie sow rneisen." Said Henry's wife talking on the phone as she walked through the back door of the saloon.

"Oh shit!" Brandy said out loud as she tried to hurry to pull her pants up.

Henry's wife cut the lights on and saw Brandy and Henry in the room. She dropped her phone and started screaming words Brandy couldn't understand.

"Tran Thoa he sai hi nim!" Yelled Henry's wife in a rage.

He knew he was caught and started yelling something back to his wife in the same language.

"It's not what it looks like." Brandy tried to explain, not knowing what the two of them were yelling amongst each other.

Brandy, still exposed, reached down to pick up her purse, but when she raised up, Henry's wife stabbed her in the neck with a sharp nail file.

"Ugh!" Grunted Brandy as she fell to the floor holding her neck. She laid on the floor leaking like a slaughtered hog.

Henry took the file from his wife and stabbed Brandy repeatedly in her upper body until she was no longer moving. Brandy was dead. What Henry was telling his wife is that Brandy followed him to the back and tried to rape him. Henry's wife hysterically called the police and reported that a transsexual tried to rape her husband, but she came in time to attack the suspect and he-she might be dead. While his wife was on the phone with the police, Henry put the crack and the pipe in Brandy's purse. The police arrived and found Brandy dead with her pants down.

When they saw her penis, they also bought the story that Henry provided his wife with. Detectives, CSI, and the news people came to the scene. Henry deserved an Oscar Award for Best Actor for his performance with the detectives. His wife, not knowing any differently, was still crying in the shock of what had happened.

"Damn chumps are going crazy around this muthafucka. " Said Detective Lewis who had been on the force for over 20 years.

"Yeah, I see. Looks like the chump was about to fuck the shit out of lil dude." Said Detective Sampson laughing.

"Get the punk's purse and see if he's got an ID or a cell phone on him." Lewis ordered Sampson.

Sampson retrieved Brandy's ID and found out her real name was Brandon Santos. Then he got Brandy's phone which didn't have a lock on it; so Sampson was able to go through it to find out if Brandy had any family. However, Sampson couldn't place any of the contacts as family, so he started going through the recent messages and found himself getting sick in the stomach from all the homo sexual pictures it contained.

"I couldn't find anything related to a family. But he seems to have had a lover." Sampson informed Lewis who was busy puffing on a cigar.

"Call him." Lewis ordered.

Sampson dialed the number and heard, "You have reached the voice-mail of Robert Smithers Jr.---beep---'' sounded Robert's voicemail.

"Yeah. This is Detective Sampson with the Las Vegas homicide division calling you in concerns of a Mr. Brandon Santos. Please call me back as soon as you get this message" Said Detective Sampson on Robert's voicemail.

Chapter Six

Tina looked at the clock and it read 9:14 p.m. She was super high and bored so she decided to throw on some clothes and go out dressed in a skin tight Black Chanel body dress and Jimmy Choo heels, Tina grabbed some cocaine from the box and left her condo heading to the "Blue Velvet."

On the way to the club, Tina couldn't resist the urge she'd been having to call Robert ever since the cocaine put him on her mind. Of course Robert gawked at Tina every time he saw her at the firm. Sometimes he even threw slick shots at Tina, blowing her kisses. But Tina's loyalty always remained with Nicole, so she acted as if she didn't see Robert do the shit he did. She just thought of him as a disrespectful muthafucka.

Now Tina didn't give a fuck about Nicole, and she was about to take her husband away from her. When she pulled into the club parking lot, she called Robert, but got no answer. Maybe he's busy or with Nicole's old fucky ass, thought Tina. Then her phone rang.

"Hello handsome." Tina answered.

"Who is this?" Asked Robert already intrigued.

"Uhhh, you hurt my feelings! This is Tina, and you don't even know my voice?" Tina said sounding sad and dejected.

"Tina from my law firm?" Asked Robert, trying to make sure of whom he was talking to.

"Yes. Tina from your law firm." Tina replied.

"Oh, beautiful. I'm sorry. I had no idea whose number this was. Is everything okay?" Robert said with sympathy.

"Yes, everything is okay. I just pulled up to the" Blue Velvet" to have a drink. My day was hectic. Why don't you come by here and have a drink with me?" Tina invited Robert.

"I just got off the plane, but I can be there in thirty minutes." Robert explained, not giving a fuck if Nicole was right beside her. He was not about to miss this opportunity. All he could think about was Tina's fat ass.

"Okay Daddy. Don't keep me waiting." Tina said flirtatiously. "I won u t, sexy." Robert replied. They hung up. Tina sniffed a few lines of cocaine and went inside the club.

♦ ♦ ♦

Robert quickly grabbed his luggage and headed for his car while thinking of so many things he would like to do to Tina. Robert then began checking his text messages and voicemails as he drove to the club" There were no texts from Nicole nor his other women, so he checked his voicemails. When he heard the message from Detective Sampson he wondered,

"Who the fuck is Brandon Santos?" Not yet putting two and two together. He called the detective back.

"Detective Sampson speaking." Sampson answered.

"Yes. This is Robert Smithers Jr. and I had a message from you about a Brandon Santos." Replied Robert.

"Oh, yes. Mr. Smithers. We found him stabbed to death about two hours ago after he allegedly tried to rape someone." Sampson informed Robert.

"But sir, I don't know a Brandon Santos." Robert told the detective.

"Maybe you know him as something else, because he's a transsexual." Simpson informed Robert.

"But sir....." Robert stopped in the middle of his sentence as his heart hit his big toe. The phone dropped to the floorboard. Robert couldn't believe his ears. Feeling sick to his stomach, he quickly pulled over to the side of the road. Robert opened his door and began vomiting, gasping for his breath. He felt more stupid than he did sick. Finally catching his breath, Robert shut his car door and picked up the phone from the floorboard.

"Hello? Hello?" Said Robert.

"Are you okay buddy?" Sampson asked while laughing.

"Yes, yes sir. Is that all you wanted with me?" Robert said stuttering.

"Yeah buddy. Don't worry. Shit happens!" Sampson said laughing hysterically before hanging up.

Robert pulled back onto the road and headed toward the club in disbelief. The kissing, touching, the fucking in the ass, what the fuck!?" thought Robert as he slapped the dashboard with his hand. Two minutes later, Robert arrived at the "Blue Velvet."

Once he parked, Robert sat in the car in disbelief of what he had done. A tear fell from Robert's eye, from the agony he was experiencing. His phone rang bringing him out of the horrible thoughts of him and Brandy.

"Hello!" He answered.

"Where are you at, baby'?" Tina screamed over the music, sounding like she was having a ball.

"I'm outside." Answered Robert.

"Well? Are you gonna come in?" Tina asked with sarcasm. "Yeah. I'm on my way in now."

Robert sat in his car for a couple more minutes, trying to get himself together. He was gonna need psychiatric help to block out the thoughts of Brandy. He entered the club and saw Tina sitting at the bar. As soon as he walked up to Tina, she jumped from her seat giving Robert a seductive hug.

"Damn, Daddy. You looking good!" Tina told Robert as she stepped back and checked him out. Robert couldn't believe how Tina was acting like she had been wanting this forever.

"You look fantastic yourself, Beautiful!" Robert complimented Tina.

Tina turned her back to Robert, letting him see her fat ass, teasing him. They took a seat at the bar and had a drink over some small talk. Tina could tell something was wrong with Robert because he seemed to keep drifting off into space.

"Are you okay?" Tina asked Robert.

"Oh, yes. I'm fine. I just have a lot on my mind." Explained Robert.

"Come on. We're gonna have some fun tonight!" Tina grabbed his hand directing him to walk with her. She led him to a booth in the back corner of the club where they sat down at.

Tina then waved over a waitress and ordered champagne and a thousand singles. Robert then handed the waitress his Platinum Visa and he smiled at Tina. Tina stood up from her seat and sat in Robert's lap.

"You can relax u Daddy. Your wife fired me today." Tina lied, but it sounded fly.

"Why?" Asked Robert, being caught off guard by Tina's statement.

"Some bullshit. You know how bossy she is."

"Don't worry about that shit, baby. Let Big Daddy take care of you." Robert told Tina.

Tina smiled and pulled the cocaine from her breast area. She untied the bag u dipped her fingernail into the cocaine and sniffed it up her nose. She planned to get Robert high so she could manipulate him. She knew Robert was lame and would do anything for some ass.

"What is that?" Robert asked Tina as she dipped her finger nail into the cocaine again.

"It's just, ah, a little something to make you feel better when you've had a bad day." Tina told Robert.

"Here. Try some Daddy!" Tina said while offering him some by putting her finger nail to the bottom of Robert's nose.

"Go ahead." Tina said applying peer pressure to Robert.

Robert needed to escape from the thoughts of Brandy and the previous night, so he closed his eyes and sniffed the cocaine up his nose. By the time he raised his head and opened his eyes, his face was numb. He sat back in his seat and started feeling like Superman.

The waitress returned to their table with their order. Tina poured their drinks, never getting out of Robert's lap. She put Robert's glass to his lips and he drank. I got his ass now, thought Tina as she looked at Robert, who was stuck from the effects of the cocaine. Tina drained her glass of champagne and leaned back to speak into Robert's ear.

"I want you, Daddy. I've been wanting you! I just didn't know how to tell you." Tina said into Robert's ear as she nibbled upon his lobe.

Robert was in the clouds and he surely wanted Tina also. Very, very, very much to be exact. Tina stood from Robert's lap and waved over two dancers who came over and immediately got on their job. With ass shaking, titties bouncing, and pussy in every direction, Robert was having the time of his life. Tina waved off the dancers so she could hypnotize Robert. She knew exactly what she was doing. She continually fed him cocaine and champagne. Tina introduced Robert to a life on the wild side.

Chapter Seven

Miquel had been thinking about his future all day. It was now time for him to make decisions that would set him straight for life. He even took the initiative to change his phone number. He didn't want any distractions or anything side tracking him from what he had planned. Earlier, after he had thoroughly cleaned his house, he called and invited Nicole over for dinner. Of course, she accepted the invite, so Miquel went grocery shopping.

Miquel was about to get his grown man on for Nicole. He had a mission to accomplish and he'll be damned if anything stood in his way. Miquel knew how to play the game to get what he wanted from a woman. He even vowed to himself not to fuck Nicole until her and her husband were not living under the same roof. Miquel is a firm believer that a woman only wants what she can't have.

Therefore, if he wanted things to go his way, he couldn't afford to think with his dick. Even though he would love to penetrate between Nicole's thick thighs and feel the wetness of her nectar, Miquel knew he would have to stay focused and not get caught up in the heat of the moment.

Nicole made it over around nine o'clock that night. She and Miquel chowed down on homemade bacon cheeseburgers and fries, which she had requested for Miquel to cook. They had Mountain Dew to wash it down with. The two of them laughed and talked during their meal. Nicole loved Miguel's sense of humor. He managed to keep a smile on her face the whole time. After dinner they sat back on the couch and watched the movie Sugar Hill while being snuggled against each other exchanging kisses between scenes.

Nicole felt so good being held by Miquel. There was a sense of being wanted and a sense of being secure when she was with Miquel. Even though he was younger than her husband, Miquel was so much more mature. Nicole was falling in love with Miquel after knowing him for only two days. She fit in his arms and chest as if she were his missing puzzle piece.

She's so soft and smells so good, thought Miquel as he ran his fingers through Nicole's hair. He loved the way he could run his fingers through her natural hair without feeling a sew-in or any other additives. She's a pure, natural woman, thought Miquel and he started smiling.

"What are you smiling about?" Nicole asked Miquel.

"You make me so happy." He told her. Nicole felt the words Miquel spoke to her. She was happy that Miquel really felt some type of way about her.

"You make me happy too, baby!" She told Miquel.

They embraced in each other's arms and shared a passionate kiss. Miquel felt his manhood begin to rise. No sex, thought Miquel and he broke their embrace.

"It I s getting late I baby." Miquel told Nicole as he looked at the clock which read 12:07 a.m.

"I know." Said Nicole in a whining voice.

They got up from the couch and Miquel walked Nicole to her car holding her around the waist, kissing her on the neck.

When they reached her car, Nicole turned around and Miquel took her into his arms, squeezing her tighter than a pair of vice grips. "I really enjoyed tonight with you, Beautiful!" Miquel told Nicole as he squeezed her ass. When Nicole didn't respond, Miquel stepped back to look at her. She raised her head and Miquel saw a tear running down her face.

"What's wrong, Beautiful?"

"Nothing. You just make me feel so special." Nicole told him. "You are special, and I won't change."

"Thank you, baby." Said Nicole. Then they hugged and kissed again before Nicole got into her car and drove off.

◆ ◆ ◆

Nicole was on her way from leaving Miguel's house when she thought about the fact that Robert hadn't tried to contact her. She logged into the Spy App on her phone that told her the exact location of Robert's phone. Nicole had discovered the app a year ago when Robert kept constantly lying about his whereabouts. The Spy App readings showed that Robert was in downtown Nashville.

Nicole decided to go and see just where Ol' Robert was at 12:30 am. She drove down Second Avenue and saw his car outside the "Blue Velvet." If she would have been paying closer attention, she would've noticed Tina's car right beside Robert's. To her recollection, Robert was to afraid to party in this type of environment. He would rather be at home on his computer looking at porn or out cheating on Nicole with a blue-eyed blonde. But after seeing the pictures from Vegas, Nicole couldn't be so sure of Robert anymore.

Nicole found a parking space and parked. While Nicole walked to the entrance, she tried to remember who or where she had heard about this club from. She pushed the thought to the back of her mind as she stepped foot inside the entrance door dressed in a tight fitting yellow Prada sweat suit and Prada slippers.

"Damn baby. Ain't seen you here before. You comin' to work?" The security guard asked Nicole as he gawked over her body.

"Nah. I just wanted to get out of the house. This is my first time here." Nicole said smiling as she handed the $20.00 admission fee.

"Damn baby, you good. Go on, enjoy yourself." Said the security guard flashing his gold teeth acting like he was the boss declining Nicole's money.

"Thanks!" Said Nicole, then she walked to the bar.

Nicole sat at the bar and ordered a frozen virgin margarita. As she sipped her drink, two strippers walked up and sat down beside her at the bar. They began talking loudly to the bartender over Gucci Mane and Chris Brown's song "Tone It Down" blasting from the speakers.

"Ya'll hoes getting money on this slow ass week night, ain't ya?" The bartender said to the strippers.

"Hell yeah, girl. That bitch Tina, who used to work here got some nigga over there tipping good." Said one of the strippers.

Nicole damn near choked on her drink when she heard what the girl had said. She had not seen Tina, so she slowly scanned the club from where she was seated.

"Oh, my God." Said Nicole, but no words came from her mouth as she laid eyes on Robert and Tina on the backside of the club.

Robert was throwing money on Tina while he drank champagne straight from the bottle. Nicole had never even seen Robert act in such a manner. Tina was all over Robert, grinding her ass into his crotch while he slapped money on her ass. Nicole had seen enough, so she hurriedly left the club before either of them saw her.

Nicole drove away from the club refusing to shed a tear, but they were hard to fight back.

She had constantly given Robert her all. Only for him to constantly show her he was ungrateful for anything she had done for him. Before Miquel, Nicole had never touched any other man during their marriage. No matter how many times Robert showed Nicole that her loyalty meant nothing to him, she still remained loyal to him and their marriage. She hated to admit it, but Nicole was emotionally torn due to the fact that Tina was involved.

She treated Tina so good, only for Tina to thank her in the worst way. Tina knew how bad Robert had treated Nicole because Nicole had poured her heart out to Tina. Tina had a motive the whole time, use me to steal Robert. A stinky bitch, thought Nicole. She had trusted Tina with the secrets of her marriage only for Tina to use them against her now.

As Nicole pulled up to her home, tears started falling down from her eyes. She sat in the car with her head leaning on the steering wheel crying like a baby. After a few minutes of sobbing, Nicole raised her head and wiped her face. Then she sucked up her snot and spit it out the window. Getting out of the car and walking in the house, Nicole thought of how she was going to immediately start looking for a building to start her new law firm. Fuck Smithers & Smithers! I don't want shit to do with the last name, thought Nicole as she covered herself with a blanket and fell asleep on the couch.

Chapter Eight

Charles had been calling Tina for about the past two hours, but he wasn't receiving an answer. He was pissed off at the fact that she was costing him money. "This bitch don't know who she playing with, do she?" Thought Charles as he sat outside the "Blue Velvet" in his car at 1:00 a.m. snorting cocaine. He got out of the car and walked towards the club entrance. He saw Tina's car in the parking lot.

"What up, Son?" The security guard greeted Charles as he walked into the club.

"Shit. Koolin'!" Charles responded, as he paid the entrance fee.

Charles stepped inside the club scanning the room. He soon spotted Tina all up on some trick ass nigga. Charles sucked his teeth while he rubbed his chin. So many thoughts were rushing his mind about approaching Tina and snatching her ass up by her neck. He decided on his better judgment by taking a seat at the bar, even though he wanted to go slap the shit out of Tina. Charles ordered a drink and then sent the waitress to tell Tina that he needed to see her ASAP. Moments later, Tina came over smiling all drunk and shit. Charles knew she was on cloud nine.

"Hey baby!" Said Tina, reaching out to hug Charles.

"Don't 'hey baby' me BITCH! I've been trying to call you for the past two fucking hours, BITCH! "Charles growled at Tina with a menacing look on his face.

Tina knew that Charles was nothing to play with. She has witnessed him pistol whip one girl because she shorted him on his money for some cocaine. Tina immediately lost her smile.

"Charles, I'll go straight home so you can come get your stuff." Tina said half scared to death.

"Bitch, you high on my shit?" Charles questioned Tina.

"No, Charles. My friend had it with him when he got here." Tina lied, knowing that she knew better than to fuck with Charles' shit without confirming it with him first.

"So that's yo new nigga over there?" He asked Tina. "Yeah, something like that."

"So I can't get that pussy tonight?" Charles reached and grabbed her ass.

"No, Charles. We about to go to my place." Tina told Charles as she moved his hand off her ass.

"Aight Bitch! I'll be over there in the morning around eleven to get my shit, and I hope that nigga paying ya rent Bitch!" Charles growled at Tina, feeling like he got played.

"Okay I'll be there." 'Tina turned around and walked back over to Robert.

When Tina made it to Robert she insisted that they leave the club immediately.

"Can you drive to my house'? I live just around the corner."

Tina asked Robert, making sure he wasn't too fucked up to get behind the wheel.

"Hell yeah, baby. I'm right behind you!" Robert said, high out of his mind. Then he got into his car and followed Tina to her condo.

Charles sat at the bar drinking straight shots of Patron back to back. The more he drank, the madder he got, as he thought about how Tina denied him her pussy after he had paid her rent the other day. On top of that, he had missed fifteen grand because she didn't answer the phone for him earlier. Charles was now drunk, high, and pissed off. I should've slapped her face off, thought Charles as he slammed down the shot glass, breaking it on the bar countertop.

Charles stumbled out of the club and climbed into his black Audi A7. He reversed out of the parking lot with his music turned up to the max. He put his gearshift in drive and pressed the accelerator to the floor. Screeching off from the club with his music blasting, Charles ran a red light without noticing the unmarked police car on the opposite side of the road. Charles looked into his rearview mirror to find police lights dancing behind him.

"Fuck!" Charles said angrily, knowing he was under the influence. But he still pulled over. He knew he was too drunk to take the police on a high-speed chase through downtown Nashville.

The police made Charles get out of the car. They searched him and found an eightball of cocaine in the fifth pocket of his jeans. The police placed Charles in handcuffs and sat him in the back of the police car while they searched his vehicle. During the search, the police found close to an ounce of weed inside the car. "Damn." He knew he was fucked because of the five years' probation that he was already on. When the police came to the car where Charles was at, he told the officer that he needed to speak with a narcotics agent ASAP.

♦ ♦ ♦

Robert followed Tina inside her condo and they went straight to her bedroom. As soon as they reached the bedroom, Tina stripped down naked of all her clothing. Robert sat on the bed amazed by Tina's flawless figure.

"Damn. Look at this fine muthafucka here." Robert thought to himself. Tina walked to the kitchen and came back with a dinner plate and a bottle of wine. Robert's eyes were glued to Tina's body, fat her ass jiggled with every move and her brown nipples stood erect. Robert was fascinated by Tina and her body.

"Why are you so quiet?" Tina asked Robert as she broke down some cocaine on the plate.

"I'm in love!" Said Robert while he stared at the landing strip of hair that rested right above Tina's pretty pussy.

Tina stopped what she was doing, to do what she had been waiting all night to do, blow Robert's mind!

"Robert, don't say anything you don't mean." Said Tina, looking directly into Robert's eyes.

"I......... was all Robert could say before Tina placed her finger on his lips, signaling for him to shut up.

"Now stand up and take off all of your clothes. "Tina demanded, and Robert did it without any hesitation.

Tina pushed Robert down by his shoulders, sitting him on the bed. Robert's face was inches away from Tina's pussy. "Rub on my pussy." Tina ordered him.

Robert rubbed on Tina's pussy and watched her pussy drench his fingers with her wetness.

"Ohh, uum." Cooed Tina as she took Robert's fingers and applied more pressure to her clitoris.

Robert watched Tina take his fingers and then put them into her mouth, tasting her own juices. He was lost under Tina's love spell. She pushed Robert back so that he was laying on his back. Then Tina climbed on top of him so that they were in the sixty nine position. Tina dribbled her ass cheeks on Robert's face while he fucked her pussy with his fat tongue. As she rode the hell out of Robert's face, Tina put his entire small dick into her mouth.

Tina now saw what Nicole was talking about. Robert's sex game wasn't hitting on shit. He didn't even know how to correctly eat pussy, but he was really trying to.

The cocaine had Tina freaky as hell and she really wanted to have an orgasm. Tina decided to change positions so she turned around facing Robert and inserted his dick inside her pussy.

She bounced on his dick while he fucked her ass with his fingers, but Tina still wasn't getting to where she wanted to be. Too bad, because Ole Robert couldn't hold it anymore.

"Ugh, Ugh." Grunted Robert as he released his sperm inside Tina who was upset because she didn't get to get off like he did.

Tina quickly jumped off of Robert. She was pissed off that she didn't have an orgasm.

"Baby, I couldn't hold it any longer. I tried. "Said Robert pleading his case.

"It's okay. Maybe the next time you can make it happen for me, Daddy." Tina replied. Then she snorted two lines of cocaine. Tina wasn't ready for what happened next. When she raised her head from the plate of cocaine.

---BOOM!---

"Everybody down on the fucking floor! DEA!" Yelled the agents after Tina's door flew off the hinges. The agents had a search warrant for cocaine.

Tina fell to the floor, but Robert jumped out of the bed making the wrong move.

"I said get the fuck down! " Yelled the agent right before he smacked Robert across the face with his Glock 40, breaking Robert's jaw upon impact.

"Uggh !" Screamed Robert as he fell to the floor, holding his face.

The agents put Tina and Robert in handcuffs and then took them and sat them in the living room on the couch. Robert was crying like the day he came out of his mama's womb. Tina sat pinching herself to see if she was dreaming. She knew it wasn't a dream when one of the agents walked from her bedroom holding a shoe box. It was the same shoe box she had been stealing from.

Robert and Tina were transported to the Davidson County Jail for booking. Both of them were given a million dollar bond on the charge of Trafficking in Cocaine. Tina was getting fingerprinted by a deputy when she saw Charles come from the back, walking with the same agent that was at her condo.

"Charles!" Yelled Tina, causing Charles to look in her direction.

"Help me!" She cried, only to watch the agent pat Charles on the back and tell him good job.

Charles smiled at Tina then shot her the middle finger and walked out of the police station a free man.

"What the fuck is going on?" Tina asked herself.

When the police caught Charles with the cocaine and weed, he made a deal to give up his dealer so he wouldn't have to go to jail. He told the

DEA agents that he bought his cocaine from Tina and she had plenty of it in her condo. The agents used a fake search warrant and busted Tina.

Robert sat in the holding cell crying while he held his face. This was his first time in jail and he was really ready to leave. Tina had made Robert's night wonderful, only for him to end up in jail with a broken jaw. It would be hours before Robert and Tina would get interviewed by the investigators and until then there would be no phone calls. Robert remained in the cold cell feigning for some cocaine to soothe the pain of everything he had been through.

Chapter Nine

Nicole woke up around 7:00 a.m. and Miquel was her first thought, which put a smile on her face. She checked her phone and there was a message from Miquel. Missing you, Beautiful, read the message. Nicole decided to call him.

"Good morning, Beautiful." Miquel answered.

"Well good morning, Mister." Nicole was happy to hear Miquel's voice.

"What do you have planned today?" He asked her. "YOU!" She replied.

"Then hurry up and get to me. I quit that law firm. I'm at home now."

"I'm on my way." Nicole said laughing at Miquel's sarcasm. Then they hung up.

Nicole got dressed, dried her hair, and went to Miquel's house. When she arrived, Miquel had prepared a breakfast that consisted of turkey bacon, cheese eggs, pancakes, and grits with orange juice to drink. He fixed their plates and sat them on the trays sitting in front of the couch where Nicole was sitting.

"Dig in!" Said Miquel as he grabbed the remote and turned on the television.

Nicole and Miquel were taking turns feeding one another and kissing each other until they were interrupted by what was being said by the news anchorman.

"This morning DEA agents arrested Robert Smithers Jr. and Tina Adams on felony charges of Trafficking Cocaine. Suspects are now being held in the Davidson County Jail. The weather is up next." Said the anchorman as Robert and Tina's mug shots dis appeared from the screen.

"Damn baby, that's fucked up!" Miquel said to Nicole, who was smiling, which totally caught him off guard.

"I don't care." Said Nicole shrugging her shoulders.

Miquel could tell that Nicole wasn't the least bit surprised by the situation and for a reason that was unknown to him.

"Okay, baby. Are you gonna fill me in, or leave me like Ray Charles to what's going on?" Miquel asked Nicole.

"Okay honey. Look at this." Said Nicole as she pulled up the pictures of Robert and Brandy on her phone.

"That's your husband with a dick by his mouth!' Said Miquel shocked at the pictures.

"I know! That was two nights ago in Vegas, Miquel. I'm done with any and everything that has something to do with Robert.

It's over! I only want you!" Nicole told Miquel while she fought to hold back her tears.

Miquel knew that Nicole's words were real and from her heart. He grabbed Nicole and hugged her with all his might, showing her that she was secure with him.

"I only want you, babe." Miquel told Nicole, then her phone rang.

"You have a collect call from..." Is all the operator had a chance to say before Nicole hung up the phone.

"Baby, I have a couple of errands I need to run. Can I see you later?" Nicole asked Miquel, who was wondering why she hung up on the phone and why she was trying to leave all of a sudden.

"Sure thing baby! Go handle your business." Miquel told Nicole even though he felt something fishy was up. They hugged and Nicole left.

Nicole arrived at the First American Bank at 8:30 a.m. The bank wasn't open yet so she Googled real estate in the area, searching for an office building she could buy. The bank's doors opened at 9:00 a.m. and Nicole went inside. She withdrew all the money from the law firms business account and put it into an account with only her maiden name on it.

Nicole wasn't about to let the Feds take everything she had worked so hard for. She knew the Feds were gonna freeze everything with Robert's name on it. Nicole walked out of the bank with over a million dollars in cash in a duffle bag" She had also secured over 5 million dollars in an account that was in her maiden name. Nicole drove to the other side of town to meet with a real estate agent about a building she had found while waiting for the bank to open. Nicole and the agent walked into the building and Nicole was given a tour of it. The newly renovated building consisted of four very spacious offices. The building was perfect for what Nicole was gonna do with it. Nicole paid the agent $250,000 cash money for the building and the agent signed over the deed. Nicole was so happy to finally own her own office that she could work out of. She stashed the rest of the money inside the building and then left.

♦ ♦ ♦

"Yes, Jamison I know. But it's not what it looks like." Robert explained to Jamison, a lawyer from his firm.

"So why hasn't Nicole come and gotten you out yet?" Asked Jamison.

"Look. I don't have to explain shit, but if you want to keep your fucking job, then I suggest that you get your ass down here with a bondsman for me and Tina Adams." Robert said angrily into the phone.

"Will do, sir. I'm on my way."

When Robert hung up the phone, the thought about how Nicole didn't accept his call crossed his mind. Hell, she should've been here to make my bond before it got posted, thought Robert. Robert wanted to do one thing and one thing only. Finish what he and Tina started last night before they got carried off to jail. The cocaine had Robert's thought processes fucked up. All he wanted to do was freak and geek. Party! Party! Party! Robert constantly thought. He wanted to get his hands on the best cocaine money could buy. They need to hurry up and come get me out of this muthafucker, thought Robert as he started growing impatient.

Miquel sat in a McDonald's parking lot across the street from the building Nicole had just purchased. He'd been following Nicole since she left his house. He had seen her come out of the bank with a duffle bag. The same duffle bag he watched her take inside the building. Miquel knew Nicole had just bought the building because he watched her take the "For Sale" sign from the parking lot of the building and throw it into her car right before she pulled off.

Miquel couldn't stop thinking about the duffle bag.

"Fuck following Nicole, I need to see what's in that bag." Thought Miquel. He pulled around to the back of the building and he got out of the car. He made sure nobody was looking before he kicked the back door off the hinges.

One good kick and the door flew open. As soon as Miquel walked into the front office of the place, he saw the duffle bag sitting in plain sight. He unzipped the bag to find nothing but blue Benjamins staring him in the face. Sweat formed on Miguel's forehead and he felt a rush go through his body. Miquel zipped the bag up and threw it over his shoulder. He then propped the back door up and left.

When Miquel made it home, he went straight to his bedroom and dumped the money out of the bag onto his bed. Count up, count up, thought Miquel. He counted over eight-hundred-thousand dollars. His mind began to race with so many thoughts about what to do. Do I say fuck Nicole? Should I give her money back? Is this the lick I've been waiting for? Stop! Get yourself together, Miquel told himself. Then he put the money back into the bag and called Nicole.

"Hello!" Nicole answered.

"Hey baby. Are you busy?" Miquel asked her.

"No. I'm pulling up at the house to pack my stuff." Said Nicole as she pulled into the driveway of her house.

"Oh yeah! Where you going?" He asked.

"Home to my man, if that's okay with you!" Nicole said sarcastically. Miquel smiled as he heard her answer.

"I can't wait for you to get here, Beautiful."

"Okay, baby. After I leave here I am going by the law firm to get my personal files and then I'm coming straight home." Explained Nicole sounding like she was in a rush.

"Okay, baby. I love you."

"I love you more." Said Nicole and they hung up.

Miquel threw his phone on the floor and buried his face into his hands, feeling guilty about stealing Nicole's money. He really felt like Nicole was true to him and only him. "How am I gonna explain to her what I've done?" Miquel asked himself.

Robert and Tina walked out of the police precinct at 11:17 a.m. Wednesday morning. Jamison gave them a ride to Tina's condo. The security at Tina 1 s building told her she wasn't allowed inside the building until the detectives gave the landlord the green light to allow her to come back. Tina's feelings were hurt. Robert hugged her.

"Don't worry, baby. I'll take care of you. "Robert told her. "You promise?" Tina asked Robert in her pity voice.

"Yes, baby. I promise. I got you!" Answered Robert, wanting Tina to believe him.

Tina knew that she had Robert totally obsessed over her and she was gonna take full advantage of the situation. They got into Robert's Bentley Coupe and drove off.

"How is your face, baby?" Tina asked Robert as if she was really concerned.

"It's okay, but I need some stuff." He told Tina.

"Okay, boo. I got you. Turn left at the next light." She directed.

Tina directed Robert to her home girl, Meko's house. When they pulled up at Meko's, Tina called her and she came outside. Meko gave Tina an eightball of cocaine. Tina told Meko what had happened to her and Meko told Tina not to worry about paying her for the cocaine.

"Thanks girl!" Tina thanked Meko.

"You welcome. Be careful!" Meko told Tina, then she went back inside her house.

As soon as they pulled off, Tina dipped her long fingernail into the bag. Then she put her cocaine piled nail to the bottom of Robert's nose and he sniffed away as he drove. Robert felt his pain start to evaporate and his magic power was coming back.

"Better now, Daddy?" Tina asked Robert as she reached over and grabbed his crotch.

"You always make me feel better, baby." Robert told Tina as he drove home.

♦ ♦ ♦

Jamison called and notified Nicole that Robert and Tina were most likely headed in her direction. Nicole hurried and put the rest of her belongings into the trunk of her Malibu that was sitting on the side of the house. She decided she was gonna leave in the same car she was driving when she met Robert. Nicole got inside her car and looked into the rearview mirror to begin reversing from the side of the house, but stopped when she saw Robert's Bentley pull into the driveway. When she heard Robert's car doors close, Nicole began reversing from the side of the house.

Robert and Tina were standing in the driveway about to walk into the garage, when they saw the Malibu converge from the side of the house with Nicole driving. Nicole blew the horn and waved bye to them. Robert grabbed a huge rock from the flower foundation and threw it at the car.

---BOOM!---

The rock hit the hood of Nicole's car as she drove off. "Stinky bitch!" Yelled Robert. Then he turned around and walked towards the house. Nicole drove away a happy woman. As she drove down the interstate, a thought crossed her mind and she laughed. Nicole pulled up the pictures of Robert and Brandy on her phone and forwarded them to Tina's phone. Before Nicole could raise her head, "Beep, Beep, Beep!" was all she heard before she got hit by an eighteen wheeler truck. It seemed as if time had stopped as Nicole's car flipped in the air. When her car hit the ground, it flipped another three times before stopping with Nicole unconscious.

"Someone call the cops! Help! Somebody call an ambulance!" Screamed on lookers who pulled over to see what was going on.

Nicole was stuck inside her crumbled car unaware of everything that was going on.

Tina stepped out of the shower admiring her new home. She noticed Nicole had taken a lot of her belongings and wouldn't be returning. Tina was claiming her new spot as the queen of the castle. As she dried off, the message alert on her phone sounded off. What could this bitch possibly want texting me, thought Tina when she saw the message was from Nicole.

Tina opened the message and couldn't believe her eyes. What the fuck?! There is no way in hell this shit is real! Robert is one sick punk muthafucker! Tina thought to herself as she looked through the photos.

"Baby, did you find everything okay?" Robert asked Tina as he stepped into the bedroom to find Tina looking distraught.

"Robert, what the fuck is this Nicole sent to my phone?" Tina asked him with her face frowned up.

"Let me see that, baby!" Said Robert, taking Tina's phone from her to see what she was talking about.

As soon as Robert looked at the phone he gagged and threw up everywhere. He dropped Tina's phone as he ran to the bathroom vomiting. He was as sick as the pictures were. Tina sat on the edge of the bed in disgust.

Damn faggot! Robert is a damn ding dong! Tina thought to herself.

This explains why Nicole left without a fight! And I thought I was doing something! Well, since I know his deepest secret, he can get ready to get juiced. Punk ass dude might let me fuck him with a strap-on! Thought Tina as she walked to the bathroom where Robert was on his knees in front of the toilet. Tina wet a rag.

"Baby, I accept you for whatever you've done." Tina told Robert as she dabbed his head with the wet rag to cool him down.

"It's not what it looks like, Tina. I didn't know she was a man! I swear!" Pleaded Robert.

"Come on, baby! Get up! We ain't gonna cry over spilled milk.

"I need some clothes." Tina told Robert as she pulled his arm for him to stand up from the floor.

Robert got up and gave Tina a T-shirt and some sweatpants.

Then they left the house to go shopping, but got stuck in traffic on the interstate which was backed up due to a wreck. Once they made it closer to the actual wreck, Tina noticed the crumbled car looked a lot like Nicole's car.

"Baby, that looks like Nicole's car." Said Tina, looking at the car being loaded up onto the wrecker truck.

"Fuck that bitch! She can die and go to hell for all I give a fuck! Baby, you are all I care about." Robert told Tina.

His words put a Kool-Aid smile on Tina's face. She felt like she had accomplished something.

◆ ◆ ◆

Charles knocked on the back door of his partner, Dante's, apartment.

"Who is it?" Asked a female voice. "It's Charles!"

The door opened and Charles was met by Dante's girlfriend, Meko, and her Glock. Charles stepped inside the apartment.

"Dante in the living room." Meko pointed towards the living room area.

Charles was hoping that Meko walked in front of him so he could lust over her fat ass, but he had no luck. Charles walked into the living room where Dante and two of his young shooters were counting money.

"What's up, fam?" Said Dante as he stood up to give Charles some dap.

"Shit bruh! I got a lil problem." Said Charles.

"Lay it on me, Homie!" Replied Dante.

"I got robbed by this bitch and her nigga. Charles lied. "So you ain't got the money for the brick I fronted you?"

Dante was not happy about what Charles was saying.

"Nah bruh, they took everything!" Declared Charles.

Meko was standing right behind Charles listening to the lies as they left his lips. She had already got the 4" from Tina. She knew Charles was trying to play her man. Meko didn't bother Dante with the news she'd gotten from Tina because when she returned inside the house from talking to

Tina, Dante was in the kitchen cooking crack. Meko knows not to bother Dante while he is cooking.

"Bruh, just give me a couple ... "Charles stopped talking when he felt Meko's pistol poking the back of his head.

"Babe, what are you doing?" Dante asked Meko, confused of what she was doing and why.

"This right here." Said Meko, which were the last words Charles heard before, "BOOM!"

Meko blew Charles' brains all over the living room.

Chapter Ten

Miquel sat at home wondering why Nicole hadn't called or came to his house yet. He called her phone, but he got her voice mail. So many thoughts began to rush Miquel 1 s mind. Is she okay? Maybe she's just busy! I'm trippin' I haven't known this woman for a week and she already got my mind gone, thought Miquel.

Miquel had always been the player type who really didn't give a fuck about a female nor what she was doing. But Nicole had him gone over her. He really did have feelings for her. He called her phone once more, and again he got the voicemail instead of her.

It was a hot summer night in June when Nicole got off from her job at Starbucks at 8:00 p.m. She climbed into her Pontiac Sunfire and tried to crank it, but it wouldn't start. She popped the hood to see if she could fix her problem. Greg pulled into the parking lot of Starbucks to catch his play when he noticed this thick sexy, caramel lil baby standing at her car with the hood up. He pulled right in front of her in his classic old school Oldsmobile Ninety Eight, which looked like it just came off the show room floor.

"Excuse me, lil mama! Do you need some help?" Greg asked Nicole, who was glad someone had pulled up and offered her some help.

"Yes. If you don't mind. My car won't start." Nicole replied.

Greg threw his car in park and jumped out looking fresher than kids do on their first day of school. He had on matching blue and yellow Ralph Lauren hat, shirt, shorts, and socks. His shoes were all white low top Air Force Ones. Nicole always gazed at a man's shoes when she was analyzing him. When she made it to Greg's face, Nicole was attracted to him like a fly is to shit. He stool 5'0", medium build, with smooth chocolate skin and wavy hair that was freshly cut into a temp fade. Damn. He is fine as hell, Nicole thought to herself.

"Let me take a look at it, Beautiful." Greg told Nicole. Then he took a peep at the objects under the hood. He wiggled a few wires while Nicole stood on the side watching.

"Go try to start it now. He told Nicole.

Nicole got in the car and turned the ignition. Her car cranked straight up. She was relieved and happy as hell that her old Sunfire had not given up on her. She got out of the car and walked back to Greg, who was closing her hood.

"Thank you so much! What do I owe you?" Nicole asked Greg.

"Your name!" Greg replied.

For the next fifteen minutes, Greg and Nicole sat outside of their cars conversing. Nicole could tell that Greg sold something because he had two phones that were blowing up.

Greg was really feeling the college girl who also worked. He even knew some of her people. Even though Greg was 31 and ten years older than Nicole, she was still very interested.

"Call me tomorrow at noon, lil baby, and I'll get that problem fixed for you." Greg told Nicole who agreed and they exchanged numbers before they departed each other.

Nicole thought about Greg all that night and vice versa, Greg thought about Nicole. The next evening came and Nicole called Greg. He told her to meet him at Lamar's Auto Mart. When she pulled up at the lot, she spotted Greg talking to what appeared to be a car salesman. Nicole walked up behind Greg and tapped him on the shoulder. When Greg turned around and saw Nicole, he melted like shortening in a hot skillet. She was gorgeous, wearing a thin yellow sun dress that revealed enough of her body to make any man's imagination run wild.

"Can I have a hug, Beautiful?" Greg asked Nicole as he took her soft body into his arms and squeezed her gently. He released their embrace and stepped back.

"Here you go!" Greg handed Nicole a set of keys.

"What's this, Greg?" Nicole was confused.

"Your problem is fixed, with no payments." Stated Greg as he pulled out the title to the barely used Chevy Malibu, giving it to Nicole.

Nicole held the keys and title to her chest. She was lost for words. Greg let out a slight laugh.

"You can thank me later! I gotta get my son to his mom's.

He's in the car waiting for me." He informed Nicole.

"Are you serious, Greg?" Nicole asked, still shocked that Greg had just given her the keys to a basically new car and told her it was hers.

"It's yours, Beautiful. You deserve some reliable transportation to get you to school and work." Greg told Nicole. Then he kissed her on the cheek and walked to his car.

Greg blew Nicole a kiss as he drove off. Neither Greg nor Nicole knew that would be the last time they laid eyes on each other for a long time.

"Damn, Pops! Who is she?" Greg's son asked as he looked at Nicole's thick, pretty legs.

"Stand down, youngin! That's ya pops' new lil' meat." Greg said, smiling.

An hour after Greg dropped his son off, he was set up by the Feds, and didn't get out of jail. He had no way to get in touch with Nicole, but she still crossed his mind from time to time.

The thought of Nicole always made Greg smile. Nicole sometimes thought about Greg and the thought of him also made her smile.

"She's smiling!" Nicole heard the nurse say.

Nicole slowly opened her eyes and realized she was at the hospital. She noticed she was hooked to an IV. She tried to raise up, but she felt a sharp pain in her head.

"Ahh." Nicole winced.

"Oh no ma'am! Lay back down!" The nurse ordered Nicole. "Mrs. Smithers, you've suffered from a mild concussion that had you in a deep sleep for the past two hours. u, The nurse informed Nicole.

Nicole then remembered the wreck. Trying to send that bitch Tina those funky ass pictures and she got into a wreck because of it, thought Nicole.

"I'm sorry, Sir. But your card has been declined." The cashier at Bloomingdale's told Robert.

Robert had never heard those words before. He looked back at Tina and shook his head. He pulled out another debit card from his wallet and handed to the cashier.

"Try this one. II Said Robert, as he smiled at Tina.

"I'm sorry, Sir, but this card has been cancelled. " Said the cashier.

"Something must be wrong with your machine Sweetie. I have plenty of money!" Robert proclaimed.

"I'm sorry, Sir. But it's your card!" Replied the cashier. "You know what? Fuck you! Come on, baby!" Robert said, grabbing Tina by the arm and marching out of the store.

Robert and Tina were walking out of the store when his email alert went off on his phone. He stopped walking and checked his e-mails which read insufficient funds, and that his account had been cancelled.

"I'm gonna kill that bitch!" Yelled Robert, infuriated at Nicole.

"What's wrong, baby?" Tina asked Robert, seeing that he was steaming mad.

"That bitch stole my money from my bank accounts!" Robert huffed, about to cry.

Tina suddenly felt so stupid. Why did I think Nicole would just leave Robert without taking anything? I knew better than that. Now here I am with a broke faggot who can't do shit for me, thought Tina.

"So, what are you gonna do? Because I have no clothes and we are damn near out of sugar?" Tina asked Robert.

"I'm gonna find this bitch and make her give me my money back!" Robert told Tina as they got inside his car and headed home.

By the time they made it to the house, Tina's high was coming down, and she was hungry. So while Robert called the bank and argued, Tina made herself a sandwich. As she sat on the couch chewing her sandwich, Tina looked at the pictures on top of the fireplace of Robert and Nicole. Before she knew it, she started crying. She was hurt and felt so stupid. All she had to do was play her cards right, but Tina couldn't control her emotions and feelings. Now she has a major felony and she is jobless. Her life seemed to be crumbling right before her eyes. Tina covered her self with a blanket and closed her eyes, trying to block the nightmare out. Hopefully, when I wake up, this will all be over, thought Tina.

♦ ♦ ♦

It had been three hours since Miquel last heard from Nicole and he was beginning to worry about her. He had called her phone over twenty times, only to reach her voicemail. Miquel also called the law firm, but there was no one there either. Miquel had to do something he'd never done when looking for someone. He called the jail.

"Davidson County Metro Jail." Said the jailer.

"Yes, I am trying to see if you have a Nicole Smithers in custody?" Miquel asked, feeling like a complete lame for calling around the city looking for Nicole.

"Hold on, Sir. Let me see." Replied the jailer and put Miquel on hold for about two minutes.

"No, Sir. We don't have a Nicole Smithers in our system."

The jailer informed Miquel and ended the call.

Where else could she be? Thought Miquel as he flopped down on the couch. His mind drifted off to when he was thirteen and his mother was looking for his Pops. His mother was worried to death until his Pops called from the hospital explaining how he had been shot and robbed by some niggas in Memphis, Tennessee. The hospitals, thought Miquel. He began to call each hospital, determined to find the woman who he u d known for so little time, but seemed to care so much about.

It must have been the luck of the draw because he found out where Nicole was at on the first hospital he tried. The receptionist told Miquel the room number Nicole was in and he couldn't get out of the house fast enough.

♦ ♦ ♦

Robert stood over Nicole as she lay in the hospital bed asleep from the heavy medication the doctor had given her. Robert was at home arguing with the bank manager when the hospital called and notified him that Nicole had been in an accident. Robert flew to the hospital like he had wings. As he stood over Nicole, his mind raced with so many things he would like to do to Nicole, like choking the shit out of her to wake her up. Robert wanted to torture her to tell him where his money was at, so he could get back to Tina whom he left at home on the couch asleep. Tina had Robert's mind going crazy. She was the finest woman he 9 d ever laid hands on, and he wanted to spoil her in every way he could. Besides, Tina was still by his side even after the fact that she found out he'd slept with a man.

Robert loved Tina for that.

I gotta play my cards right in order for her to give me my money back, thought Robert as he slightly ran the back of his hand across Nicole's forehead. Nicole slowly opened her eyes. Anxiety set in as soon as she saw Robert standing over her. Nicole felt like Lucifer himself was standing over her. She felt misfortunate to be in a hospital bed with Robert standing over her. Small beads of sweat started to form on Nicole's forehead.

"Robert, please .leave!" Said Nicole in a soft tone of voice as a single tear drop ran down her face. Nicole closed her eyes and said a short prayer. "Lord, please deliver me from this situation. Amen."

Before Nicole could open her eyes, she heard the room door open and Miquel walked in.

"Baby, are you okay?" Asked Miquel as he walked to Nicole's bedside. He leaned down and kissed Nicole, acting as if Robert wasn't even in the room.

"Yes, baby. I'm fine." Answered Nicole as she silently thanked God.

"What the fuck is this faggot doing here?" Miquel asked Nicole as he mean-mugged Robert. Miquel was ready to tear into Robert's ass like he was a fresh pack of Newport's. Especially when he noticed how uncomfortable Nicole was.

"I'm her husband. And who are you calling a faggot?" Robert said to Miquel, trying to act tough.

"Robert, just leave!" Yelled Nicole.

Miquel started walking around the bed towards Robert. Robert got nervous and started fidgeting in his pants pocket. Before Miquel could get in arms reach of Robert, Robert pulled out a .38 snug nose revolver and pointed it directly at Miquel's chest.

"I'm not going anywhere until I get my fucking money!" Robert said through clenched teeth. His adrenaline was rushing like never before and he could kill Miquel if he needed to.

Still lying in the bed, Nicole found what she was searching for and pushed the call button for the nurse to come in the room. Moments later the room door opened.

"Yes, Mrs. Smithers?" Said the nurse as she entered the room, but dropped her clipboard and froze in place when she saw Robert with his gun drawn on Miquel.

"Nicole, give me my damn money so I can leave!" Begged Robert.

Miquel was mad as hell that there wasn't shit he could do. He wanted to see if Robert was really about some gangsta shit, but Miquel was no dope and decided that a mental battle would be more successful than a physical battle since Robert had a gun pointed at him.

"Just give him the money, Nicole. It's not worth our lives." Miquel told Nicole.

Nicole took the string with a key on it from around her neck and handed it to Robert. Still pointing his gun at Miquel, Robert took the key and started back peddling to the door.

"What does this go to?" Robert asked Nicole.

"1423 West Nocturne. The sign to the building is in the back of the BMW, if you don't believe me. The money is in the building inside a black duffle bag in the front office. Now leave Robert! Please! "Said Nicole in a low tone of voice.

Robert tucked the gun under his shirt and darted out of the room as fast as he could possibly manage. Robert thought for sure Miquel would be on his heels, but he was wrong.

"Ma'am are you okay?" Miquel asked the nurse.

"Yes. I'm fine. They teach us how to handle hostage situations when we first start working here. Mrs. Smithers, you can go home."

Your test results came back negative. I have you a prescription for your headache and the doctor will come in in the next 10 to 15 minutes to discharge you." The nurse told Nicole who wasn't paying her any attention because she was too busy kissing Miquel.

"I love you Nicole." Miquel said between kisses.

"I love you Miquel."

Miquel ended the kiss because he knew he had to hurry up and get Nicole away from the hospital. He knew Robert wasn't gonna find what he was looking for. Miquel went and got in his car. He pulled to the door of the hospital where Nicole would emerge from. Five minutes later, Nicole came out. As Miquel drove, he tried to come up with a plan to either tell Nicole about the money or get rid of Robert.

Chapter Eleven

The ringing of Tina's phone awakened her from sleep. It was her landlord calling to tell her it was okay to go back to her condo but she had thirty days to be moved out. Even though she had to move, Tina was happy she could go home for the moment. She felt so out of place at Robert's house. Tina was tired of being anywhere near Robert's gay ass.

"Robert!" Tina yelled out loud, but she didn't get a response.

Tina got off the couch, opened the front door and took a look outside. She saw that Robert's car was gone. She went upstairs to Robert's room and decided to snoop around to see what she could find of value. Tina knew that Robert had so much going on that he wouldn't notice if anything was missing. When she reached the bedroom dresser, Tina saw a jewelry box.

She opened the box to find Nicole's wedding ring, which had to be worth at least $50,000. There was also a his and hers Rolex set worth about $20,000 as well. Tina called a Uber service. While she waited for the Uber to arrive, Tina kept herself busy by loading all the expensive threads from Nicole's closet into a garbage bag"

"Beep! Beep!" The Uber honked his horn.

Tina grabbed all the merchandise and got into the Uber.

"Take me to the nearest pawn shop. "Tina ordered the driver.

Tina rode in the back of the Uber thinking about a master plan to get her shit together. She figured she could sell the jewelry for a nice amount to get a head start. She was gonna also start back dancing because she refused to be a broke hoe.

Tina also made her mind up that she didn't want anything to do with anyone associated with Nicole unless Miquel came to his senses.

◆ ◆ ◆

Robert walked through the building looking and searching for a duffel bag that wasn't there. After twenty minutes of searching, he came to the realization that the bag wasn't there. Nicole had played the shit out of him once again. Robert got into his car and went to his bank. He felt so in need for money that he took out a loan for $25,000 just to blow it on Tina. With the money in his possession, Robert happily returned home. Once inside his house, he noticed that Tina was gone. He called her phone but got the voicemail.

Robert was tired of being played. He had had enough. He went upstairs to his room to get ready to shower. On his way to the bathroom, he stepped on a sharp object that pierced his foot. Robert bent down to see what it was and found that it was an ear- ring. He went to place the earring in the jewelry box on the dresser but it was gone.

Robert took a look into Nicole's closet and saw that the clothes that Nicole didn't take were missing too.

"Stanky bitch!" Yelled Robert, knowing that Tina had stolen the belongings and had left him.

I'll be damned she gonna get away with this shit, thought Robert. He dialed Tina's number, but after two rings, it went to the voicemail. Robert smiled because he had a good idea of where she would be and where he could find her tonight. Robert hit the shower. When he got out of the shower, Robert was relaxed and a little tired so he set his alarm and took a nap.

◆ ◆ ◆

Once at home Miquel got Nicole settled in. She was banged up a little from the wreck and her head had started back hurting. She was also glad that Miquel had insisted that they stopped to get her medication and something to eat. As Nicole sat up in the bed eating, Miquel sat next to her staring at her.

"Baby, you look so pretty." He told Nicole.

"Baby, stop it! I look so rough!" Said Nicole as she playfully punched Miquel in his arm.

"I swear it seems like I've seen you somewhere before I met you at the office." He told Nicole while staring at her.

"I doubt it because I never go out." She replied as Miquel wiped Ranch Dressing from the corner of her mouth.

"Maybe you don't, but I never forget a face."

Nicole finished eating and called her mom. While she was on the phone, Miquel got lost in his thoughts, thinking about his problem. He had the money that he was sure that Robert wanted.

I gotta come up with a plan and fast, thought Miquel before Nicole said something to him.

"What's on your mind, baby? " Nicole asked Miquel when she noticed he was staring up at the ceiling.

"Oh nothing baby! Just thinking about my pops. He gets out in the next few weeks." Miquel lied.

"Oh! Well, I can't wait to meet him."

◆ ◆ ◆

Tina finally made it to her home from the pawn shop, where she had been for the last hour wheeling and dealing with the owner about the jewelry. He only gave her $10,000 for the jewelry because he knew it didn't belong to her. The owner also promised Tina, that if the merchandise was reported stolen, she would have no worries since she gave him such a great deal. Tina agreed, knowing that the jewelry didn't belong to her and she needed the money. The transaction was done off the record so Tina didn't have to present any ID or contact number.

When Tina walked inside her home, she was quickly reminded of the previous night when she looked at all the shit that was thrown everywhere by the police. She wanted to cry, but she didn't have the time to cry over spilled milk. Tina dumped the bag of clothes she had taken from Robert's house out on the floor. She sifted through the bag for an outfit to wear to work. She found a white Prada body dress with the tag still on it and threw the rest of the clothes into the bag. Tina decided to call Meko to see if she wanted the rest of the clothing from Nicole's closet.

"What it do?" Said Meko when she answered. "Hey girl! What you doing?"

"Shit girl! What up?"

"Not shit! I got a whole bag of new Prada, Gucci, and Fendi shit that u s your size." Explained Tina.

"What do you want for it?" Meko asked Tina.

"Shit, just look out for me on the "Booger Sugar. "

"Okay, bet! I'm at the house."

"Give me about an hour. I'll stop by there before I go to work."

"Cool!" Said Meko and they hung up.

◆ ◆ ◆

Greg arrived at the Greyhound Bus Station in downtown Nashville at around 7:15 p.m. He stepped off the bus, cleaner than a broke dick dog in his sky blue and yellow Ralph Lauren outfit with Polo slides on his feet. Greg didn't look a day older than the day he went to the penitentiary. As a matter of fact, he looked better. He walked to the pay phone and called his son, but the phone was disconnected. He called the number again to make sure he dialed the right number, but still got the same result of the phone being out of service. Greg only had one living relative and that u s his niece Meko. Greg's sister, Stella, passed away from a heart attack a year before Greg got locked up. Stella had one child named Mekonah, but everyone called her Meko. Meko was twenty years old when her mother passed. She had just gotten out of the Women's Prison in Knoxville, Tennessee for a stabbing she had committed.

Upon Greg's imprisonment, he gave Meko his drug connection, but under no circumstances was she to get his son involved in the drug trade. That reason being Greg didn't want to be the reason his son chose the dope game as his lifestyle. All Greg wanted from Meko was for her to deposit a hundred dollars a week into his son's bank account and send him a hundred dollars a week for his prison commissary. Meko respected her uncle's wishes to the fullest and held him down his entire bid.

Greg called Meko's phone. "Ring! Ring! Ring!"

"Who dis!" Meko answered.

"Who do you want it to be, Princess?" Greg asked her. "Aiihhh, Uncle Greg!" Screamed Meko from excitement.

Greg started laughing as the sound of Meko screaming for happiness made him happy as well.

"Yeah, Love. I was trying to sneak in on your lil' cousin u but the nigga phone off." Greg told her. "Where you at, Unc?" Meko asked him.

"I'm downtown at the Greyhound bus station, but I'm about to walk down to this lil spot I've been hearing about that's down the street called the "Blue Velvet." Greg informed Meko.

"Give me thirty minutes, Unc, and-I'll be there." Meko was eager to see her Unc.

"Okay, Love. I'll be there." Said Greg and they hung up. Greg walked down two blocks from the bus station and he was at the club.

Chapter Twelve

After Nicole ate and took her medication, she drifted off to sleep. When Miquel saw she was out for the count, he got her address off the pill bottle and slipped out of the house in all black to go take care of Robert once and for all. Ever since Robert pulled his pistol out on him at the hospital, all Miquel could think about was killing his ass. Miquel pulled down the street from Robert's house and parked. He was gonna simply kick in Robert's front door and kill Robert and Tina. Too bad for Tina, but her ass was about to die right along with her new gay friend. Miquel had planned the perfect double homicide in his mind. He slid a ski mask over his face and cocked the pistol. Just when Miquel was about to open his car door, he saw Robert pull out of the driveway. Miquel decided to follow Robert from a distance to see where he was going.

◆ ◆ ◆

Tina had called Meko to see if she was at home, but Meko told her she was pulling at the "Blue Velvet" to meet her uncle. So Tina went straight to the club.

"Oh, shit! These hoes is in trouble tonight!" Said Big Mane, the Security Guard 1 when he saw Tina walking through the entrance rolling her dance bag behind her.

"You already know how I do it, Big Mane!" Tina said to him as she walked through, throwing her ass, killing the white Prada dress she was wearing.

Tina was on her way to the dressing room when she spotted Meko at the bar talking to some sexy ass nigga. Tina walked to the bar where they were seated.

"Damn bitch! You wearing that dress ain't ya?" Meko complimented Tina when she walked up.

"Just something a little light." Tina got a good look at the man sitting beside Meko.

"This is my uncle Greg, who just got out." Meko introduced Greg to Tina after she realized Tina was gawking over her uncle.

"Hi! I'm Tina" Tina said, blushing. Damn, this nigga fine as hell, thought Tina.

"Nice to meet you, Sexy!" Greg told Tina. This little muthafucka here finer than a muthafucka, thought Greg as he observed Tina 1 s pretty face and curvaceous figure.

"I gotta have her tonight! Shit, it's been eleven years." Greg leaned over and told Meko in her ear. Meko started laughing.

"Let me holla at you, Homie!" Said Meko as she jumped off her stool leading Tina to the restroom.

Once inside the restroom, Tina pulled out the clothes she had for Meko. Meko loved the clothes and gave Tina a half ounce of cocaine in exchange for the clothes.

"Is this straight?"

"Hell yea, girl! But what's up with your Uncle though? He's fine as hell."

"Shit, he just got out today. So I guess he's all yours." Meko said, downplaying the conversation and not letting Tina know that Greg wanted her as well.

"Do me a favor and see if he wants to fuck with me. If he does, then I won't work tonight. Ya feel me'?! "Said Tina, and the both of them burst into laughter.

"Shit, come on! I got you, Homie!" They left the restroom going back to the bar where Greg was at.

When they made it back to the bar, Greg reached out and grabbed Tina's hand, pulling her to him. Tina felt a tingle run through her body from Greg's touch.

"I ain't gotta say shit! Girl, Unc don't play!" Meko told Tina who was blushing.

Then Dante entered the club with one of his young goons and joined them at the bar. Dante and Greg gave each other love.

"This is a small blessing from me and Meko. Thanks for every thing, Unc!" Dante told Greg as he handed him the key to a new S550 Benz which was parked outside. Dante then took the MCM backpack from off his back which contained $30,000 inside it and handed it to Greg.

Greg took a look inside the bag and approved the gift.

"That's love, Nephew! I really appreciate that! Thanks a lot, ya hear?" Greg told Dante as he dapped him up.

"That's the least we can do, Unc. You showed us major love!" Meko told Greg then hugged and kissed him on the cheek.

Dante called over a waiter and requested a VIP booth with five bottles of Don Julio and two thousand singles. They all went to the VIP section and started partying. Greg and Tina were really attracted to one another.

♦ ♦ ♦

Miquel trailed Robert, who pulled up at the "Blue Velvet."

He watched Robert park, get out of the car, and go inside the club. Miquel was mad as hell that his plan didn't go like he wanted it to. He damn sure wasn't about to wait on Robert to leave the club. Miquel decided to abort his mission and go back home.

♦ ♦ ♦

Robert stepped inside the club, ready to make it rain and do his damn thing. He saw Tina's car outside so he knew she was there. Robert walked to the bar and wasted no time ordering a bottle of Moet and a thousand singles. He scanned the club to see if he saw Tina. She wasn't in sight, but the strippers from last night were.

One of the girls recognized Robert from last night. Not wanting to step on anyone's toes, she went to the VIP section where Tina was sitting in Greg's lap.

"Can I holla at you for a second?" Vanilla said loud enough for Tina to hear her over Gucci Mane's "Trap God" blasting from the speakers.

"I'll be right back, Baby!" Tina told Greg in his ear and she got up from his lap to see what Vanilla wanted.

"What's up, Boo?"

"The guy you were with last night is at the bar." Vanilla informed Tina who immediately became bug-eyed.

"Did he ask you where I was?"

"No. I just saw him and I came straight to you. What's up with him though?" Vanilla asked.

"If he has any money, he will spend it. But please don't tell him that I'm here." Tina said in a serious tone.

"Okay, Boo! I just didn't wanna step on anybody's toes." Replied Vanilla.

"Nawl, girl, he ain't my nigga! Get your money." Tina told Vanilla. Then she went back to sit on Greg's lap. Vanilla left the VIP section heading straight to Robert who was still sitting at the bar alone.

◆ ◆ ◆

Stacy Austin, a.k.a. Vanilla, stood 5'7" and weighed 160 pounds. Her high yellow complexion, fat ass, and D-cup breasts, which was all accompanied by tattoos, was enough to make any man drool. Not to mention while at work she never covered her big brown nipples. Vanilla knew how to run the game and she loved to play the game. Whether she's up on her shit or down on her luck, Vanilla is the type of bitch that will never change. Robert noticed Vanilla's thick yellow ass walking in his direction and he was ready to get to know her.

"Hi, handsome!" Vanilla spoke to Robert, whose eyes were glued to her large breasts.

"Well hello to you, sexy!" Robert replied.

"Would you like a private dance?" She asked Robert. "I would be delighted." He answered.

"Follow me!" Vanilla ordered him. Robert grabbed his champagne and followed Vanilla to the private dance section of the club, located in the back.

◆ ◆ ◆

Tina watched Robert and Vanilla from the VIP section as she stood beside Greg. When she saw them go into the private dance section, Tina excused herself to go to the restroom while Greg was occupied tipping a stripper. She had come up with a plan to make sure Robert was occupied and not thinking about her. Tina found Chocolate, the other stripper from last night and pulled her into the restroom.

"What's up, Boo?" Asked Chocolate.

"Give this to Vanilla and tell her it will keep that nigga she with spending. He got down with me for the first time last night." Tina told Chocolate, handing her the bag of cocaine she had gotten from Meko.

"Ok, Boo!" Said Chocolate.

"Y a'll both can get that nigga. He's a major trick." Tina informed Chocolate.

"Okay, Boo. Thanks. I got you!" Replied Chocolate and they both left out of the restroom.

Tina made it back to the VIP section to find out Meko and Dante were leaving the club.

"Take care of my uncle, bitch!" Meko yelled over the music to Tina.

"He's in good hands, girl!" Tina yelled back as she sat in Greg's lap.

"So, baby. Are you ready to leave?" Tina asked Greg as he watched Meko and Dante go down the stairs.

"Yeah, Baby. Let's get out of here."

◆ ◆ ◆

Chocolate and Vanilla had Robert in the private dance section working him good. Robert was now on another level. His magic power had kicked in as soon as he hit the "booger sugar." Robert asked Vanilla how much it would cost him for her and Chocolate to go home with him. She told him for $1,500 a piece they would both go get dressed right then and follow him home. Plus, the cocaine was included. Robert agreed.

When Vanilla first got Robert to the private dance section, he pulled out $10,000 with the bank band around it. She wondered how she was going to be able to get it, but now she knew. Vanilla didn't let Chocolate in on her little scheme either.

◆ ◆ ◆

Miquel took off his clothes and climbed into the bed with Nicole, who was sound asleep. He was glad his plan didn't' work. What was I thinking? I was actually about to kill that nigga when he already dead" Hell, I got Nicole and the money! Why not let the nigga kill himself?! Thought Miquel as he ran his fingers through Nicole's hair. She felt his touch and scooted closer to him, laying her head on his chest.

Chapter Thirteen

Greg and Tina checked into the Embassy Suites. Greg took off his shirt as soon as they entered the room. At 42, Greg was still eye-candy. He stood 5'" and weighed 190, which was all muscle. Tina was amazed by his physique. Her eyes were glued to his chocolate skin. The creases in his abs and pelvis made her pussy moist. Oh my God, thought Tina.

"I'm about to shower, baby." Greg told Tina. "Okay. I'll be waiting!"

Greg stripped down butt-naked right in front of Tina. He took his time neatly folding his clothes and putting them on the vacant table next to the television. Tina was astonished at how fine Greg was. From his head to his feet, his body had definition. Tina stared at Greg's dick as it swung, being six inches on the soft. She wondered how much it would grow once she placed it in her warm mouth. She watched Greg's ass cheeks as he walked to the bathroom. Tina could see his dick and balls hanging from the back view. Tina's pussy started tingling and wanted some attention.

She couldn't take it any longer, so she quickly stripped out of her clothes and went into the restroom. Tina slid back the Shower curtain to find Greg smiling at her.

"I thought you might join me, Said Greg as Tina stepped into the shower.

Greg and Tina took one another's tongues into their mouths as the shower ran over them. Greg cupped Tina's ass and picked her up. He held her up with his strong arms while they kissed. It had been a long time since Greg had sex, so his dick was already erect. Tina held onto Greg's neck as she felt him enter inside her lava hot pussy. With one pump, Greg stuffed everything he had inside Tina.

"Oooo yess, Daddddyyyy!" Moaned Tina feeling like she was about to cum.

It was as if Greg had forgotten that pussy felt so good because he was about to nut and he had just gotten started. He tried to fight the sensation dancing inside the head of his dick, but it was no use.

"Ahhh shiitt, ugghh!" Yelped Greg as he exploded inside Tina, filling her up with his semen. The nut was so intense that Greg's body jerked simultaneously sending Tina into an orgasm.

"I'm cummin, Daddy!" Screamed Tina while Greg held onto the shower wall to keep from falling.

♦ ♦ ♦

Robert, Vanilla, and Chocolate were all in the hot tub at Robert's house. Vanilla sat on the opposite end of the other two. She noticed how much Chocolate had changed since she saw what kind of car and house Robert had. Chocolate was acting like a fly does to shit. Vanilla had only one thing on her mind and that was hitting Robert for everything she could. Vanilla didn't have all night anyway. She had to be home at 2 a.m. Her boyfriend, Des, was there waiting for her. It seems like Chocolate is trying to start a relationship with this nigga, thought Vanilla as she mixed up a special treat for Robert and Chocolate. Vanilla knew what she had to do. She held up one of her big pretty titties and poured some of the cocaine she had mixed onto it. Robert and Chocolate floated in her direction and started sniffing the cocaine up their noses. Vanilla knew if they kept sniffing at a fast pace, they would soon be too high to see what was coming their way.

Robert had two bitches at the same time and you couldn't tell that nigga shit. He was sniffing cocaine of Vanilla's titties and then licking the residue off of them. He was going extra hard. Robert and Chocolate seemed to be having a get high competition. The shit he had sniffed hit him fast and hard, making him lean back against the wall of the hot tub. He was stuck. The cocaine seemed to have the same effects on Chocolate's groupie ass, because she was also stuck. Vanilla was okay because she didn't sniff any. If Chocolate wouldn't have been so much of a groupie,

Vanilla would've hipped that bitch about the heroin she had mixed in with the cocaine.

Robert and Chocolate were speed-balling. They were super high from doing all the dope Vanilla mixed up. Hell, they were so high that they hadn't noticed that the water had drained out of the hot tub. Vanilla laughed at their stupid asses as she lit up a blunt and began rummaging through Robert's room. It only took ten minutes of searching before she found $15,000 in the bedroom dresser drawer. Vanilla took another eight grand from Robert's pants pocket. Next, she hurried and gob ddi'essed to leave. Damn I'm glad I drove my own shit, thought Vanilla as she placed the remainder of the cocaine on the side of the hot tub.

"Where you going?" Chocolate asked Vanilla, then she nodded back out.

Vanilla tried to wake her up, but her attempt was useless. Chocolate was high out of her mind. Vanilla looked at Robert who was also nodding uncontrollably and she decided it was best for her to leave them as they were. Vanilla smiled, happy that her mission was complete. Chocolate better get her ass up out of here before this nigga wakes up and realizes he's been robbed, thought Vanilla before she grabbed her purse and left.

♦ ♦ ♦

Greg and Tina lay in the bed after an explosive sexual escapade. They conversed and got to know each other mentally. Tina was shocked when Greg mentioned that Miquel was his son. She quickly informed Greg that she had just met Miquel the past Monday at work. Tina shared with Greg the events in her life from the time she met Miquel up to the present. She had Greg's full attention. She started crying while she was pouring her heart out to Greg.

Greg didn't know if he was getting older or just getting soft, but Tina had definitely intruded on his heart. From everything Tina had told Greg, it seemed to him that she had been through a lot.

"It's gonna be okay p Beautiful." Greg assured Tina as he rocked her like she was a baby while she cried.

On the other hand, Greg was glad to hear that his son landed him a successful lawyer. He couldn't wait until the morning came so he could surprise Miquel. But for now, Greg needed to rest because Tina had fucked his brains out.

♦ ♦ ♦

Robert and Chocolate seemed to be able to control their nodding at around the same time. Robert climbed out of the waterless hot tub and went into the bathroom to take a shit. Chocolate acted as if she was still nodding until Robert closed the bathroom door. Then she jumped out of the hot tub and began putting on, her, clothes and getting ready to leave. After she put on her clothes, she needed to find her keys but couldn't. She searched high and low but she still couldn't find them. Robert heard movement inside the bedroom and quickly wiped his ass to get up from the toilet. When he opened the bathroom door he saw Chocolate who seemed to be looking for something.

"Are you looking for something? " Robert asked Chocolate as he crept up behind her.

Chocolate damn near jumped out of her skin from the sound of Robert's voice.

"Yeah, my keys! Have you seen them?" Replied Chocolate. "No, I haven't. And where is your friend?" Asked Robert as he noticed Vanilla wasn't in the room.

"She left!" Said Chocolate as she continued to look for her keys.

Robert walked over to get his pants to get his phone. When he reached in his pants' p6cket to get the phone, he noticed that his money was gone. Robert went straight to his drawer for his other money, but it was gone also. Robert grabbed his gun and walked straight over to Chocolate. He pointed his gun at her while she was looking for her keys under the bed.

"Where the fuck is my money?" Growled Robert.

"I don't." Chocolate stopped mid-sentence when she raised her head up from under the bed and saw Robert's pistol pointed at her head.

"Where is my god damn money?!" Screamed Robert, fuming mad.

Chocolate was too scared to speak.

"Oh. So you not gonna say shit" Said Robert, then he grabbed Chocolate by her hair and put his pistol to her head.

Chocolate knew her life could end if she didn't tell Robert something.

"I don't know unless Vanilla stole it from you". Said Chocolate as a tear fell from her eye.

"Since you don't know anything, you' r e gonna take me to her.

Call her and see where she is." Robert ordered Chocolate. Chocolate feared for her life, so she did exactly as she was told.

"What's up, bitch'?" Vanilla said laughing when she answered the phone.

"Nothing. Where you at?" Chocolate said dryly.

"I'm at home." Said Vanilla, sensing something was wrong by the way Chocolate was talking.

"I'm on my way over there." Chocolate said, still talking dry.

Vanilla didn't say anything and began punching numbers on her phone. Chocolate looked at her phone and started dialing numbers on her phone also.

"Hello! Hello!" Said Chocolate.

"Yeah, bitch! I'm here! Come on!" Said Vanilla, glad to see that Chocolate picked up on the code of her punching numbers into the phone.

"Okay!" Replied Chocolate and she hung up the phone relieved that Vanilla knew something was wrong.

"Come on. You're driving." Robert told Chocolate and they went and got inside her car.

Chocolate drove for fifteen minutes held at gunpoint until they pulled up in front of Vanilla's house.

"You stay in the car! " Robert demanded. He had in his mind that he would go knock on the door and when Vanilla opened the door, he would draw his gun on her and make her give him his money.

"Give me your phone." Robert ordered Chocolate, and she handed him the phone. Robert shut the power off on Chocolate's phone and tossed it back to her as he got out of the car. Robert ran up to Vanilla's house and knocked on the front door with his gun in hand.

---KNOCK KNOCK KNOCK---

Was the last thing Robert heard before...

---PLOW PLOW PLOW PLOW PLOW---

Robert's body jerked every time a bullet inserted him. After being hit several times, Robert fell to the ground and started flopping like a fish on dry land. What Robert didn't know was that Des was on the other side of the door waiting for him with an AK-47. Vanilla had told Des everything that was going on and he said he would take care of it. So when Robert knocked on the door, Des looked through the peephole and saw that Robert had a gun. Des politely stepped back from the door and let his chopper loose on Robert. As soon as Chocolate heard gun shots, she frantically sped off, going to her house.

Vanilla called the police and reported that someone tried to home invade on her. She told them her boyfriend saw that the man had a gun, so he shot the man through the door. The police and detectives arrived minutes later. They got statements from Des and Vanilla resulting in Robert Smithers Jr's death being written off as justifiable homicide.

Chapter Fourteen

Nicole woke up around six o'clock in the morning. Miquel was still asleep when she went into the bathroom and showered. When she got out of the shower, she dried off and walked into the bedroom where she lotioned her body while she gawked at Miguel's naked body. Nicole felt her pussy moisten as she thought of some of the things she would like to do to Miquel while he slept on his stomach with his dick laying between his legs. She couldn't resist the temptation anymore and started kissing Miquel on the back of his neck.

Miquel woke up and tried to turn over, but Nicole put force down on his shoulders letting him know to stay put. This was her show and she was the star. Miquel didn't resist as Nicole kissed down the center of his back down to his ass cheeks. Miquel slightly flinched from the rare feeling of his ass being kissed. Nicole grabbed Miquel's dick from between his legs and began stroking it with her hand while she licked on his ass cheeks.

Miquel was thinking the unthinkable. Am I supposed to like this? thought Miquel as Nicole grabbed his hip with her free hand and pulled upward, directing him to hike his ass up. He followed her lead. Miquel found himself positioned face down, ass up. Once in position, Nicole began licking Miquel's asshole while she continued to stroke his dick.

"Ummm slurp!" Moaned Nicole as she licked Miquel's asshole.

Miquel was confused at first, but he couldn't deny that fact of what Nicole was doing felt very good. Nicole stopped licking his asshole and took his dick into her mouth.

"Damn, baby. Shit!" Said Miquel as he received head from the back. Nicole slurped away at Miguel's dick like it was the last popsicle on the 4th of July. Miguel's dick was harder than it had ever been in his life. He didn't know that his dick reached back that far. Nicole took Miguel's dick out of her mouth and started stroking on it with both of her hands. Then she stuffed her face between his ass cheeks and started back licking his asshole.

Nicole was so turned on that she had pussy juice running down her thighs. She was ready to be fucked. She let Miguel's dick free and brought her face out of his ass. Next, she grabbed Miquel by his waist area instructing him to roll over on his back and he did so. Miquel's dick stood straight up in the air as Nicole brought their mouths together, entangling their tongues. Nicole reached up under herself, grabbing hold of Miguel's dick and inserted it into her extremely hot love box.

"Ooooh Miquel baaabby!" Cried Nicole as she had an orgasm upon the entrance of Miguel's rock hard cock.

"Baby, you feel so fucking good." Miquel told Nicole as he felt her hot creamy pussy tighten on his dick.

Nicole bounced up and down on Miguel's dick repeatedly as the two of them experienced ecstasy.

"Ahhhh hmmmmm ! ! I'm about to cum again! "Screamed Nicole.

Miquel grabbed both of Nicole's ass cheeks and started fucking her from the bottom as hard as he could.

"Baby, I'm about to nut!" Said Miquel.

"Ye sss, yesss, yesss!" Screamed Nicole, shaking as she produced another orgasm. Miquel drove everything he had inside Nicole, making her body shiver.

"Ugh ugh ugh!" Grunted Miquel as he released his load inside Nicole.

Nicole collapsed onto Miguel's chest while they both tried to regain their breath. Miquel's mind was blown and his ass was wet. He had never experienced anything like what had just occurred.

◆ ◆ ◆

Greg and Tina were in the middle of some hot early morning sex when they were disturbed by the constant ringing of Tina's phone.

"Baby, you might wanna get that." Greg told Tina as she bounced up and down on his pole.

"Damn." Huffed Tina in frustration as she climbed off Greg to answer the phone.

"What?!" Yelled Tina, mad as hell when she answered the phone.

"Tina. Dude dead." Chocolate said in a low voice.

"Who? What dude are you talking about?" Tina asked, confused about what Chocolate was talking about.

"The guy from the club!" Explained Chocolate.

"Oh shit! For real?" Tina replied, now fully attentive as to what Chocolate was saying.

"Google the Six O'clock News and call me back." Chocolate told Tina.

"Okay!" Replied Tina and they hung up.

"Is everything okay, Baby?" Asked Greg, sensing something was wrong by the look on Tina's face.

"Yea, I mean no. Shit, I hope so." Answered Tina. "Didn't you say that you know where your son lives?" Tina asked Greg.

"Yeah. Why?" Greg said, changing the expression on his face.

"We might need to go by there because the girl he's messing around with, her husband just got killed last night. Said Tina.

Before Tina could finish her sentence, Greg had jumped out of the bed and started putting on his clothes.

♦ ♦ ♦

Chapter Fifteen

Delhia Carter rode in the back of the limo along with her personal body-guard, Steve. This was her first time in the United States since she caught her husband, Robert, fucking another man. The day she caught him it took everything on God's green earth for her not to kill him. She decided with better judgment and divorced Robert. She told her son, Robert Jr., to pack his clothes because they were leaving that very day, but he threw a hissy fit and said he wanted to stay with his father. Delhia granted her son his wishes. That day Delhia left the United States for Jamaica.

Now over twenty years later, she was back in Nashville to bury her only child. Roberta, Delhia's ex-husband's sister, called her at two a.m. with the news of her son's death. As soon as she heard her son was killed, Delhia and Steve caught a red-eye flight from Kingston, Jamaica to Nashville, Tennessee. At 54, Delhia didn't look a day older than 35. She's gorgeous. Women envied her at 5'4"and 145 pounds of an hour glass figure with beautiful yellow caramel skin. Most people often misjudged her by thinking she was boujee, but Delhia's a sophisticated lady by appearance and a gangster at heart. The story she'd heard behind her son's death didn't sit too well with her and she was going to get to the bottom of things.

Delhia's limo pulled in front of Robert's house. Steve led Delhia to the front door and rang the doorbell, but nobody came to the door. Steve twisted the door knob and the door was unlocked so he and Delhia went inside.

"Is anyone home?" Steve yelled out loud, but nobody responded.

Steve had his Desert Eagle in his hand and ready for action.

They took a walk through the house downstairs and then went up-stairs. When they entered Robert's room they noticed how disfigured and out of place things were inside the room.

"Look like he had some type of party in here." Said Delhia as she picked up an empty champagne bottle off the floor.

"Yes ma'am it does. Look at this." Steve told Delhia as he held up a bag of cocaine that he got off the side of the hot tub.

"I know damn well that nigga hadn't started fucking wit that shit." Declared Delhia, not believing what she was seeing.

"I ain't saying he was, but that's what it .looks like." Said Steve, trying not to pour kerosene onto a fire.

"Come on. Let us go down to the law firm." Said Delhia.

♦ ♦ ♦

"Damn, baby. These cheese eggs are good as fuck!" Miquel told Nicole as he munched down on the breakfast she had cooked.

"Yo ass just hungry!" Said Nicole u and they both started laughing.

---RING!---- RING! RING!---

"Baby, see who that is?!" Miquel told Nicole who got up from the couch wearing nothing but a t-shirt and walked to the door.

"Who is it?" Asked Nicole. "It's Greg!" Answered Greg.

"Open up, baby. that's my Pops!" Miquel told Nicole and she opened the door. When the door opened, Greg and Nicole's eyes met; Neither of them could believe it. They stared at each other for what seemed like to be a lifetime before Miquel interrupted their ogling.

"Pops! You got out!" Said Miquel as he came to the doorway to give Greg a hug.

Nicole moved out of the way so the two could reunite. What the fuck is going on? Nicole asked herself, especially when she noticed that Tina was with Greg.

"Yeah, I got out yesterday. I tried calling you, but your number was disconnected." Greg explained. He was happy to see Miquel was okay, but he also had other thoughts on his mind.

"And where did-you find her at?" Miquel said playfully to Greg, asking about Tina who turned up her nose at the question.

"Chill son. This is my friend Meko hooked me up with last night. She told me she knew you and the misses right here. And your name, Beautiful?" Greg asked Nicole as if he didn't already know.

"Nicole." Nicole played right along with Greg.

"Well, nice to meet you, Nicole! I'm Greg, Miquel's Pops!" Greg put an honest smile on his face.

"Ya'll don't just stand there. Come in!" Said Miquel, happy to see his Pops was finally out.

Greg and Tina took a seat on the love seat while Miquel and Nicole went back to their seat on the couch.

"I don't know what kind of news this may be to you, Nicole, but Robert got killed this morning around one o'clock." Tina informed Nicole.

Nicole was caught off guard by the news, but she wasn't hurt.

Robert had already been dead to Nicole. She was more shocked by Greg being Miquel's father.

"I'm sorry to hear that, Tina, but it's more of your concern than it is mine." Nicole told Tina.

"Bitch! I'll whoop your ass!" Tina jumped up from her seat, but was quickly pulled back down by Greg.

"You gotta watch your attitude little lady." Greg told Tina, looking directly into her eyes.

"Please excuse me!" Nicole got up and went into Miquel's bedroom.

Greg had to restrain his eyes from looking at Nicole's ass as she walked to the back. Damn, this is a small fucking world, thought Greg.

"Well, I don't mean to sound harsh, but the fuck nigga got what he wanted. The faggot pulled a pistol out on me yesterday at the hospital." Miquel told Greg and Tina.

They say if you live by the gun, you die by the gun." Replied Greg.

Nicole was in the bedroom laying across the bed with so much running through her mind. Why was Robert killed? Why did Greg and I have to meet again under these circumstances? Is Greg gonna tell Miquel? These are just some of the thoughts running through her mind, Nicole just wanted to disappear.

"Where's your bathroom, Quel?" Asked Greg. "Down the hall to your left." Replied Miquel.

Greg was walking to the bathroom, but stopped dead in his tracks when he looked to his right and saw Nicole laying across the bed. She was laying on her stomach with nothing on but a T shirt that had risen up, exposing her gorgeous legs and bare ass. Greg wanted her and he couldn't deny it.

"Pssst. Psssst!" Greg sounded with his mouth.

Nicole was brought out of her thoughts from the sound. She turned over and there he was standing in the hall. Greg blew Nicole a kiss which sent a sensation through her body. Greg could hear Miquel and Tina talking about what happened to Nicole's husband, so he knew he had a minute. Nicole couldn't resist smiling at the man she longed for, for over a decade.

Greg knew Nicole was a freak from everything Tina had told him, so he knew Nicole was gonna love what he was about to do. He pulled out his sleeping dick and began stroking it. Nicole watched as Greg's dick grew into a monster right before her eyes. On my god! thought Nicole as she felt her pussy throb and mouth getting wet from watching Greg play with his pole. She felt her legs open up and her finger rub her clitoris. Nicole was lost in a trance. She was feeling Greg without him touching her.

Greg quickly tucked his rock hard cock back into his pants then turned around and walked into the bathroom. Once Greg disappeared, Nicole snapped out of her trance-like state of mind and quickly got out of the bed and closed the door to the room. What the fuck am I doing? Nicole questioned herself. Miquel and Tina were talking about Robert, but the conversation took a drastic turn when Miquel saw that Tina didn't have on any panties. He felt his manhood starting to come alive when he caught a glimpse of Tina's vagina.

"Close ya legs!" Miquel whispered to Tina.

Why? You mad your daddy got this pretty pussy and you didn't?" Whispered Tina with a devious smirk on her face as she opened her legs more and parted the lips of her vagina, revealing all of her pretty pussy.

Miquel was speechless while his eyes were glued to Tina's fat clit. Tina watched Miguel's dick rise, sticking up through the thin gym shorts he was wearing.

"Yeah, I thought so!" Tina said with her lips turned up, then she sat up straight on the couch and crossed her legs.

"Damn, girl!" Miquel said in a low tone of voice as he grabbed his erection and squeezed on it.

"Give me something to drink boy!" Said Tina.

"Help ya self." Replied Miquel and he watched Tina chunk her ass from side to side as she walked passed him on her way to the kitchen. I've been in denial, thought Miquel.

"So. What's good, Quel?" Greg asked Miquel as he walked down the hall drying his hands with a paper towel.

"Nothing Pops, just trying to get things together." Miquel responded and the two started talking.

Nicole got dressed, but she couldn't find her shoes. She looked under the bed and they weren't there, so she went to the closet. When she opened the closet door and looked down, there was a black duffle bag on the floor identical to the bag she had left at the building she bought. This couldn't be the money Robert was supposed to get, thought Nicole as she bent down and unzipped the bag. Sure enough, it was the money. Nicole zipped the bag up and closed the closet. She took a seat on the edge of the bed while her brain ran a thousand miles per hour. How did Miquel get that money? Does Miquel have something to do with Robert's murder? Nicole asked herself.

Nicole sat and tried to come up with an answer to justify why Miquel had the money, but she couldn't come up with one. The one thing Nicole did know is that Miquel is a liar. Lie to me once, you will lie to me again, thought Nicole. She was tired of being lied to and anything else that had something to do with a muthafucker trying to play on her intelligence. Nicole had her mindset that she was gonna show everyone that she wasn't one to be fucked with. She went back into the closet and opened the duffle bag. Nicole stuffed her purse with as much money as she could carry, especially since it was a big purse.

Moments later Nicole arrived in the front room where everyone else was at. She took a seat on the couch a distance from Miquel. She was steaming mad. A tear rolled down Nicole's cheek and Miquel noticed that she was crying.

"Are you okay, baby?" Miquel asked Nicole but she didn't respond.

Nicole kept a straight stare on her face, ignoring Miquel.

He tried to rub Nicole's head, but she slapped his hand away. Miquel was completely caught off guard by her reaction.

"What the fuck is wrong with you?!" Miquel said in a stern tone of voice.

"Do you really want to know, Miquel?" Nicole turned to face Miquel.

Greg and Tina were on the edges of their seats in full tune to Nicole and Miguel's unfolding drama.

"You don't really wanna know what's wrong with me because you can't handle the truth, little boy." Nicole told Miquel, pushing his buttons.

"What the fuck ever, hoe! Your mad cause ya faggot ass husband got killed? Bitch! I already know! "Miquel got loud.

"Hey, Quel. That ain't .... '' Greg was cut off.

"Man, fuck this BITCH!" Blurted Miquel, not trying to hear anything anyone was talking about.

Greg dropped his head, shaking it in disgust. "Ha, ha, ha!" Nicole let out a fake laugh.

"I'm tired of mothafuckers lying to me when all I do is keep it real. " Said Nicole as she stood up.

"And that little money back there in your closet? You can have that! Broke ass nigga! You ain't shit like your daddy!" Nicole screamed out loud at Miquel.

Greg raised his head and his eyebrows. Miquel stood up fuming mad.

"Bitch, you don't know shit about me, hoe! " Said Miquel as he reached back and swung forward, slapping the shit out of Nicole.

---SMACK!---

Greg jumped off the couch and grabbed Miquel, but Miquel quickly pushed Greg off of him.

"Bitch nigga! Get your hands off me!" Was all Miquel managed to say before ...

---BLINK!   BLINK---

Greg hit Miquel with a two piece that dropped him to the floor.

"You don't hit a woman and you damn sure ain't gonna disrespect me!" Said Greg through clenched teeth.

Miquel gathered himself from off of the floor and grabbed his pistol from off the entertainment system.

"Nigga, if you ever put your hands on me again, I'll kill you and this bitch!" Miquel said heavy with his pistol pointed at Greg.

Greg stared at Miquel for a lifelong second and he knew in his heart that this was the end of their relationship.

"Come on." Said Greg, extending his hand out to Nicole.

Nicole got up from the couch and stood beside Greg. Tina stood up so she could leave with Greg, but as soon as she took her first step

---WHAM!---

Nicole hit Tina so hard in her temple that it knocked Tina unconscious and she dropped to the floor. Greg grabbed Nicole by her arm and they left out of Miquel's house.

Miquel wet a rag and kneeled down on the floor next to Tina.

He dabbed Tina's face with the rag and she became conscious. "Are you okay, baby? " Miquel asked Tina.

"Yeah. I guess. What happened?" She asked Miquel, not knowing what had just happened and that she had just been knocked out.

"Not shit. Don't worry about it." Miquel picked her up off the floor and laid her on the couch.

◆ ◆ ◆

Neither Greg nor Nicole had spoken a word since they left from Miguel's house until Greg pulled into a gas station and parked at the pump.

"I'm sorry, Greg! I didn't mean to make you and your son fall out with one another." Nicole apologized to Greg.

Greg turned to Nicole and placed his index finger over her lips indicating for her to stop apologizing.

"It's not your fault, beautiful. And he's not my biological son either." Greg informed Nicole as he stared into her eyes.

Nicole's eyes widened as she was startled by the news Greg had just shared.

"Yeah baby. He's not! That's why he got so mad when you said he ain't shit like his daddy." Greg explained.

Nicole could tell by Greg's body language that he needed to get some things off his mind. She knew just what Greg needed considering the fact that he had just got out of prison.

"Do you wanna go shopping?" Nicole asked Greg.

"Of course, Beautiful. I would love that!" Greg replied warmly and he pulled out of the store parking lot.

Chapter Sixteen

Delhia and Steve sat across the table from Jamison inside a conference room at Smithers & Smithers. Delhia was very intrigued by all the things she was learning about her son.

Jamison had informed her on how the firm had collapsed until Nicole worked her ass off day and night to get it back intact. He also told her how Robert Jr. constantly kept getting caught cheating on Nicole, which led Nicole to have a little fling with her secretary, Tina. Jamison gave Delhia everything he knew about leading up to Robert's death. He started with Nicole dissing Tina for the mail boy. Then he told her how Tina and Robert hooked up then got busted for trafficking cocaine for which he had to bond them out of jail. Jamison ended his story telling Delhia that he had not heard from Nicole since he bonded Robert and Tina out of jail. Delhia quickly realized her son had a lot going on.

"So Jamison it is, right?" Delhia asked Jamison, who was feeling like he was on that stand as a witness during a jury trial.

"Yes ma'am, it is."

"If you had to choose one person you thought would know something about Robert's death, who would it be?"

Jamison looked at Steve, then looked at Delhia.

"I would say Tina knows something because she was the last person I saw with Robert."

"Thank you for your time and cooperation, Jamison." Said Delhia cooly.

"You're welcome, ma'am. "

Jamison scrolled through his phone and wrote down some things on a piece of paper.

"Here ma'am, this might help you." Jamison told Delhia, as he handed her the piece of paper with Tina's and Miguel's addresses and phone numbers on it. Then he excused himself and left out of the conference room.

"So Steve, what do you think?" Delhia asked Steve.

"I think we need to find this Tina bitch, boss lady!"

♦ ♦ ♦

"I just want you to know that it's fucked up how you handled me last night!" Chocolate told Vanilla.

"Bitch, what the fuck you mean? If your groupie ass wouldn't been acting like you wanted to marry the nigga, you could've read the play before it happened!" Vanilla screamed at Chocolate.

"Yeah. Whatever! Can I have my cut?" "What cut? Bitch you dead! "

"For real, Vanilla?" Chocolate knew Vanilla couldn't be serious.

"Hello! Hello!" Chocolate said into her phone then she realized Vanilla had hung up already"

As soon as Vanilla hung up, she put Chocolate on her block list.

"Baby, you gonna handle ya home girl like that?" Des asked laughing.

"Hell yeah" Fuck that Bitch!" Vanilla started counting the money that she had robbed Robert for, for the hundredth time.

♦ ♦ ♦

Miquel and Tina laid together on the couch, sharing some of their deepest secrets. First Miquel told Tina about the money he had in his closet that he had stolen from Nicole. Then he informed Tina that Greg really wasn't his father. His real father's name was Tony Johnson, but everybody called him Nashville Tony. He was pimp.

One day one of Tony's bitches was supposed to turn a trick with a rich lawyer, but when the hoe and Tony went into the lawyer's home, the lawyer didn't want the hoe. Tony sent the bitch back to the car so he could talk to the lawyer. When Tony came back from inside the house, the bitch was in the car with her throat slit from ear to ear dead. Tony took it as a sign of beef from another pimp and went to dump the hoe's body in a dumpster. When he was loading the dead body into the dumpster, someone came up behind him and shot Tony in the head.

After Miquel was done, Tina told him how she was molested by her mother's husband from the age of ten until she was fourteen. Luckily, her uncle believed her when she told him she was pregnant by her mother's husband. Her uncle went to the police and they locked up her mother's husband. Tina started crying from the thoughts of her being molested. Miquel wiped her tears away.

"It's gonna be okay, baby!" Miquel told Tina, then he softly kissed her on her forehead.

♦ ♦ ♦

Delhia and Steve rode by Tina's condo, but they were informed by the desk clerk that she wasn't at home. Delhia called the numbers she had for Tina and Miquel, but didn't get an answer with either of them. Delhia went with her last option and she gave her driver the address to Miguel's house.

♦ ♦ ♦

Miquel and Tina were in the shower washing each other's body when the shower curtain flew back.

"What the fuck?" Said Miquel as he looked at the 6 1 5" 260 pound Jamaican in front of him with a big ass. gun in his hand. Tina was so scared that she couldn't even muster up a scream.

"Get out!" Steve demanded them as he aimed the gun at Miquel's head.

Miquel and Tina didn't say a word, they just walked towards the front room where Delhia was sitting on the love seat, waiting for them.

"Sit down please." Delhia told them while she fought away lustful thoughts of Tina and Miquel.

Steve picked up their clothes off of the floor and threw them to Tina and Miquel. They immediately started putting on their clothes as their eyes went back and forth between the strange man and woman sitting in the house. Miquel looked to where he had sat his gun, but it wasn't there.

"Hi! I'm Delhia and your names please'?"

"Miquel." Said Miquel as he looked at Delhia who was so beautiful to him.

"I'm Tina." Said Tina scooting closer to Miquel.

"Hahahahaha." Steve laughed.

"Well. Ain't this something! We killed two birds with one stone!" Delhia said, glad to have someone she was looking for.

Miquel and Tina were not too enthused by Delhia's statement. A worried expression covered both of their faces.

"I'm gonna make this short and straight to the point, Miss Tina." Said Delhia, causing Tina's stomach to do cartwheels from being singled out from Miquel.

"What happened to my son?" Delhia asked Tina, who knew Delhia had to be talking about Robert.

Delhia's question seemed to ease the tension in the air because Tina and Miquel felt the weight of the world lift off of their shoulders. For twenty-five minutes, Tina explained in vivid details the events which surrounded and occurred leading up to Robert's death. Delhia learned that Robert was last seen with two strippers at the "Blue Velvet." Tina even provided Delhia with Chocolate's phone number and told Delhia she could probably find her at the "Blue Velvet" tonight. Tina even apologized to Delhia for her loss. Miquel remained silent during the interrogation as he lusted over Delhia's beauty. Everyone in the room saw the lustful look in Miguel's eyes for Delhia.

"Thank you for your time and cooperation." Delhia told Tina, then she and Steve left out of the house.

Delhia and Steve were walking to their limo when Miquel came outside and called Delhia's name. Delhia and Steve turned around. Miquel walked up to Delhia and handed her a piece of paper with his number on it.

"Call me if you need me." Miquel told Delhia.

"I'll do just that, Chocolate Drop!" Replied Delhia with a wink of her eye.

◆　◆　◆

Greg and Nicole had been shopping for the past three hours. They both bought an entire wardrobe. Nicole loved Greg's sophisticated gangster swag. He made every outfit he put on look good. Greg had his own style. Every time he came out of the dressing room in a different outfit, Nicole found herself getting more and more turned on. After shopping, Greg and Nicole had dinner at Joe's Crab Shack since they both loved seafood. While they waited for their food, the couple talked about everything. Greg told Nicole about his plans of opening a high class gentlemen's club and Nicole told him about the building she'd purchased to start her own law firm.

They even learned each other's birthdays and favorite colors. Nicole realized she knew none of these things about the previous people that she had dealt with. She admired Greg's intelligence and sense of humor. Greg went as far as picking out Nicole's flaws and making jokes about them, making Nicole laugh at herself.

His character was everything any woman would want in a man. To top it off, Nicole hadn't spent a penny the entire evening because every time she tried to spend her money, Greg objected. That let Nicole know that he wasn't' after her money. They came to the conclusion that after dinner they should rent a cabin to stay in for the weekend. Nicole finished eating her last crab leg and began staring at Greg while he ate his food.

"What's on your mind, Beautiful?" Greg asked Nicole.

"I'm gonna ask you a question and I want you to be hundred percent honest with me." Replied Nicole.

"Ok, baby! Go for it!" Said Greg as he wiped his mouth and hands.

"Do you feel any type of way about me by me fucking with Miquel and Tina, that you aren't letting me know?"

Greg looked into Nicole's eyes and took her hand and gently squeezed it with both of his hands.

"Listen to me and listen good. I wouldn't care if you were a prostitute and you fucked every man you ever knew as long as you keep it real with me!" Greg told Nicole.

Those were the realist words any man had ever spoken to Nicole and it caused her to get emotional and let a tear fall from her eye.

◆ ◆ ◆

After Delhia left Miquel's house, she instructed her driver to take her to the morgue so she could see her son's body. Delhia and Steve entered the morgue thirty minutes later. When the coroner pulled out Robert's body, Delhia felt a sharp pain run through her heart as she looked at her son's swollen, dead body. Tears streamed down Delhia's face. After three minutes of looking at the body, she told the coroner to put Robert's body away.

Once inside the limo, Delhia told her driver to take her to the Holiday Inn Express in downtown Nashville. On the ride to the hotel, Delhia started feeling like she played a part in Robert's death. He would still be alive if I wouldn't have left him here and instead taken him to Jamaica with me. Delhia kept telling herself, then she drifted off in time, back to the day when she left her son's side.

It was a hot summer Friday afternoon when Delhia left her house to go get her hair done. When she pulled into the gas station near the salon, Delhia realized she left her purse at home. She planned on going shopping after she got her hair done, so it was necessary that she went back home to get her purse. She would've called her husband to bring it to her, but when she left home, he and their son were asleep from fishing all morning. Delhia got caught in lunch hour traffic so it took her close to an hour to make it back home.

Upon entering the driveway to her home, she noticed an unfamiliar Cadillac parked in the driveway which she parked behind. When Delhia got out of her car, and walked to the front door, she saw a female sitting in the passenger seat of the Cadillac. When she entered the house, nobody was in sight.

Delhia went upstairs to her son's room and Robert Jr. was there sound asleep. She walked to the other side of the upstairs and her heart dropped before she got to the door. She heard the sound of a man moaning loudly. Delhia stepped closer to the cracked door. Before peeping inside, she prayed that her husband was watching porn, but when she looked inside she saw something Entirely different. Her husband, Robert Smithers Sr., was getting fucked in his ass by some man wearing flashy jewelry. Tears ran down Delhia's eyes as she watched her husband enjoy the man enter in and out of his asshole repeatedly. She couldn't watch any longer than she already had. Delhia went downstairs and grabbed her baby nine millimeter out of her purse. She was heartbroken and enraged. On her way back up the stairs, she stopped midway and went back down to the kitchen. Delhia put the gun back inside her purse, threw her purse onto her shoulder then she grabbed a steak knife, which she put in the back pocket of the jeans she was wearing. She went outside to the Cadillac where the woman was at, smoking a cigarette and knocked on the window. The woman rolled down the window.

"Hey girl. Do you have another cigarette?" Delhia asked the woman.

As soon as the woman turned to get the cigarette out of the cup holder, Delhia retrieved the knife from her back pocket and then reached into the car and slit the woman's throat. After Delhia sliced the woman's throat, she got into her car and parked down the street. She slumped down in her seat as she waited for the man who was evidently a pimp to come from inside her house.

Ten minutes later, the pimp finally came out of the house. Delhia watched him grow hysterical when he saw the woman inside his car with her throat slit from ear to ear. The pimp jumped into the car and took off from her house. Delhia trailed him.

He made a stop at a nearby store and used the pay phone, then went to an alley near a neighborhood where prostitution was popular. Delhia parked a block over and walked to the alley where the pimp was trying to load the dead woman's body into the dumpster. She pulled her gun from her purse as she crept up behind the man and Delhia shot the gay pimp in the head. His body dropped like a sack of potatoes. Delhia placed her gun back into her purse and walked back to her car as if nothing ever happened.

Delhia drove home with the intention of getting her son and leaving that day for her hometown of Kingston, Jamaica. When she got home and woke her son up, she told him to pack his clothes because they were moving away. Robert Jr. got irate and told her he wasn't going with her. He wanted to stay with his father.

Delhia figured that since her son was about to turn fifteen, he knew what he wanted to do.

"We're here, Ma'am." Said Steve, bringing her back to reality.

After Delhia left his house Miquel got back into the shower. While he showered, Delhia ran a marathon in his mind. He closed his eyes as the hot water relaxed his muscles and he pictured himself running dick into Delhia's fat ass. Miquel found himself stroking his dick while he fantasized about Delhia. He was so lost in his thoughts that he never heard Tina come into the bathroom.

Tina walked into the bathroom butt naked to join Miquel in the shower, but was caught off guard by Miquel pleasing himself.

Here I am with all this pussy and this nigga in here jacking his dick, thought Tina as she backed out of the bathroom quickly making sure she didn't intrude on Miquel's self sex. Her feelings were hurt because she thought Miquel wanted her, but evidently he didn't. Tina went into Miquel's room and into the closet, were she grabbed the black duffle bag of money that, he told her about.

She knew time wasn't on her side so she had to hurry. Tina threw the bag over her shoulder and went to the front door. She grabbed her phone and Miquel's car keys then left the house.

Miquel was snatched out of his fantasizing by the sound of the muffler system on his car. He jumped out of the shower and ran to the front door, but it was too late. Tina saw Miquel standing in the front door butt naked as she pulled off in his car. Miquel walked hard, stomping his way to his bedroom and looked into his closet.

"FUCK!" Yelled Miquel, and punched the wall.

He was beyond mad, but all he could do was call and report his car stolen.

Tina was tired of being played with. She knew Miquel had plans of trying to get with Delhia, that's why he ran outside and gave her his number. Tina knew Miquel was more than likely in the shower fantasizing about Delhia, that's why she stole his car and money. Fuck ah nigga, and get money! Tina thought to herself, remembering the words Vanilla told her the first night she worked at the "Blue Velvet." She may have been a slow country girl, but Tina was learning the game fast.

Tina pulled into an alley a block over from the hotel she and Greg had stayed at. She ditch Miguel's car there. When she parked the car, Tina had to laugh at herself. Her adrenaline had been pumping so fast that she just realized that she was butt naked.

Luckily, she found a t-shirt and some gym shorts on the back seat of Miguel's car. She put the clothes on and threw the duffle bag over her shoulder. Then she took off walking barefooted.

Chapter Seventeen

Greg and Nicole were inside the cabin that they rented for the remainder of the week when Nicole excused herself to go to the bathroom. The crab legs she ate earlier had went to work inside her stomach. Nicole was in the bathroom taking a dump when Greg barged in on her.

"Oh my God, Greg NO!" Said Nicole, embarrassed when Greg had come in the bathroom while she was in the middle of taking a shit.

"Get out!" Screamed Nicole as she held her stomach.

"Is that how shrimp smells when it comes out of you?" Said Greg while he laughed his ass off. Nicole also laughed.

"Greg, get out!" Nicole said between laughs.

"Nope. Not until you let me hear you drop one!" Greg told Nicole.

"What? Hell no! I can't do that in front of you, now go!"

Nicole replied, not believing what Greg said and that he actually wanted her to shit in front of him.

"Well, I guess I ain't leaving." Said Greg as he took a seat on the side of the tub across from Nicole causing her to drop her head, shaking it.

"Just drop one and I'll leave." Said Greg.

"Okay, okay, okay. Hold on." Nicole told Greg, not believing what was happening then she gave her bowels a push.

---Pliib, Pliib, Pliib---

Nicole passed gas.

"A hhh hahaha!" Greg ran out of the bathroom laughing while Nicole sat on the toilet laughing herself.

Seconds later Greg came back in the bathroom naked and turned on the shower. Damn, this nigga is fine as hell, thought Nicole as she watched Greg's dick swing from side to side.

"Bring your funky ass in here when you wipe that ass!" Greg told Nicole as he stepped into the shower.

Nicole got done shitting minutes later and joined Greg in the shower. After they showered, Greg and Nicole romanced for several hours.

◆ ◆ ◆

With Steve in a different room from her suite, Delhia had some alone time. While she laid on the bed, Delhia began thinking about Miquel. It had been over a year since she had some real dick. After she stopped talking to her last boyfriend, Delhia started fucking with females, putting a strap-on to their asses, but that shit was getting old. Delhia slightly ran her fingertips across the head of her dildo then she threw it to the side, picked up her phone and called Miquel.

"Hello?" Miquel answered.

"Hi, Chocolate Drop! " Replied Delhia and Miquel instantly knew who he was talking to.

"Hi, Beautiful! What are you doing?"

"Sitting in this room, bored! Would you like to keep me company?" Delhia offered, but Miquel knew that he had to play hardball to get what he wanted.

"I would, but I gotta find that bitch Tina. She stole my money and my car."

"Don't be so petty!" I'm sending over my driver to get you now." Said Delhia and she hung up the phone. I'm a boss. I don't take no for an answer, thought Delhia.

Twenty minutes later her limo was outside of Miguel's house to pick him up. As soon as Miquel climbed inside the limo, he popped open a bottle of champagne and turned it up.

◆ ◆ ◆

When Tina made it to the hotel she rented a room for the weekend. Once she got inside the room Tina called Vanilla.

"Hello?" Answered Vanilla, sounding sad. "What's wrong with you, bitch?" Tina asked her.

"I was asleep and when I woke up Des was gone and he took my money." Said Vanilla, then she started crying.

"Don't cry girl. I got something for you. But first, me and you and Chocolate must have a sit down ASAP!" Said Tina.

"I know I shouldn't have done her like that last night. We do need to talk." Said Vanilla, feeling guilty about the way she handled Chocolate the night before.

"We gonna be straight, Boo! Call Chocolate and I'm on my way to come get ya'"." Tina told Vanilla.

"Okay. I'm at home." Replied Vanilla and they hung up.

Tina had put together a plan for her, Vanilla and Chocolate to make some money and say "fuck ah nigga!" Before she left the hotel, Tina rented another room which she stashed her money in. She left the hotel with $50,000 to go shopping with, but she wasn't going shopping for clothes. Tina went to pick up Vanilla and together they went and picked up Chocolate. Tina then called Meko.

"What it do?" Meko said into the phone.

"Shit, Boo! I need to come holler at you if you don't mind! " Replied Tina.

"Come on through. I'm at spot number two! "Said Meko.

Ten minutes later the girls pulled in front of Meko's trap spot. Tina went inside the house where she and Meko discussed Tina's plans. Meko approved of Tina's plan and they got down to business. Tina told Meko she needed ten guns with bullets and a brick of cocaine for her trial run. Meko supplied Tina's order for $35,000 and Tina left the house carrying a suitcase. Tina got in her car with the suitcase and went back to the hotel.

Once the girls were inside the hotel room, Tina opened the suitcase and dumped the contents onto the bed. Chocolate and Vanilla's eyes bulged when they saw the dope and weapons.

"What are we gonna do with this?" Chocolate asked Tina.

"We're gonna get us some money. But first we must swear on our souls that we will never cross each other out. Are ya'll in?" Tina asked the girls as she extended her hand straight out in front of them.

"On my soul, I will never cross either one of you. " Said Vanilla and she stacked her hand on top of Tina's hand.

"So let me get this right! If one of ya cross me, I get to kill your ass, right?" Chocolate asked Tina and Vanilla.

"Damn right!" They responded in symphony and Chocolate stacked her hand on top of theirs.

"On my soul, I will never cross out either one of ya'll."
Said Chocolate.

"Ice Cream Clique on three. " Said Tina looking at the other women.

"1, 2, 3, Ice Cream Clique!" They all yelled in unison.

After pledging, Tina told the other two girls about Delhia wanting revenge for her son's death. Tina had a plan to dismiss Delhia's ass. She told Chocolate and Vanilla how Delhia came to Miquel's house. She informed them that Delhia knew that they were the last people Robert was with. Next, Tina told Chocolate to be looking for an unfamiliar number to call her phone because it is Delhia's and she will more than likely want to meet up somewhere. Last, Tina shared her most prized information with the girls of how Delhia killed Miquel's father back in the day. But she doesn't know that it was Miquel's father that she killed. The only reason Tina knew was because Nicole had told her the urban myth about Robert's mother, plus Miquel had told her how his father got killed.

Tina added one plus one to get two. Tina quickly informed the girls that the myth wasn't a myth and Delhia was about that gangster shit.

♦　♦　♦

---KNOCK, KNOCK, KNOCK---

Delhia went to her room door and looked into the peephole. Miquel was standing outside her door. She opened the door and let him in.

"Come in, Handsome." Said Delhia, smiling.

Miquel shut the door and then followed behind Delhia who was wearing nothing but a robe and took a seat on the bed. Miquel noticed a dildo on top of the bed which had to be at least twelve inches long. How am I gonna compete with that muthafucka, thought Miquel.

"I see you've been busy. " Said Miquel.

"No. I was about to use him, but I thought I'd wait for you instead. vu Said Delhia as she cut off all the lights in the room except for lamp on the dresser. Miquel laid back on a pillow. He was feeling good from the bottle of champagne he drank on the way to the hotel.

"How do you figure?" Miquel was saying when his words were cut off as he raised up and saw Delhia 1 s naked body. Her 5'4, 145 pounds frame was immaculate. Her yellow caramel skin was flawless, without a scar on it.. Delhia 1 s pretty brown nipples stood erect on the tip of her c-cup breasts and her vagina was pubescent, but neatly outlined. Miquel literally slobbered from the mouth.

"Finish your sentence, please." Delhia told Miquel who was speechless.

Steve woke up from his sleep sweating profusely, feeling like something wasn't right. He grabbed his gun off the night stand and ran next door to Delhia's room.

---KNOCK, KNOCK, KNOCK---

Delhia threw her gown on and went to the door. When she looked into the peephole, she saw Steve and opened it up. Steve walked in.

"Steve, what's wrong and why are you sweating like that?" Delhia asked Steve who was looking like a madman.

"Don't know ma'am. But there's a bad spirit or something." Steve told Delhia.

"Boy, don't be foolish. Now go on back to your room!" She told him.

Steve looked at Miquel with a cold stare. He had bad vibes and knew that something wasn't right.

"I'll be next door if you need me, ma'am!" Steve told Delhia and then he went out of her room and went back to his.

Delhia locked the door then went and sat beside Miquel on the bed.

"Is everything all right?" Miquel asked Delhia.

"Yes, everything is fine. " Lied Delhia, her intuition had also kicked in.

Miquel reached over and rubbed Delhia's thigh, but as soon as he touched her Delhia had a vision of her shooting Nashville Tony in the head.

---SMACK---

Delhia quickly slapped Miquel's hand away from her. Miquel looked at Delhia like she was crazy.

"Hold up." Delhia stood up from the bed. "What's wrong with you?" Miquel asked Delhia.

"Nothing, I just need something to drink." She replied.

Why of all things did I just think about killing that nigga?

Delhia questioned herself as she got a bottle of water from the refrigerator.

Miquel noticed how Delhia sat at the table instead of on the bed with him after she got the water. I ain't got time for this shit, thought Miquel.

"Maybe I need to leave." Miquel suggested to Delhia who was staring at the wall.

"Yes. Maybe you do. "Delhia felt like she needed to be alone to think.

Delhia went to her suitcase and took out ten thousand dollars and then threw it to Miquel.

"That shall get you through the night and we'll get together some other time. "Delhia told Miquel who didn't say a word. He just got up and left the hotel.

On the ride back to his house, Miquel thought about where he would be able to locate Tina. The only place he could come up with that she could be at was the "Blue Velvet." She couldn't be stupid enough to go there, thought Miquel.

♦ ♦ ♦

It was eight o'clock night time when Chocolate's phone rang. The girls were parked five houses down from Miquel's house, steaked out waiting to see if Delhia might come over. Tina figured the old bitch wouldn't give them a chance by coming around, but they had to try and see if some-thing would happen.

"I think this might be her, sis!" Chocolate told Tina as she looked at the phone number she didn't recognize.

"Give it to me! " Tina reached for the phone.

"Hello?" Answered Tina.

"Hello. Is this Chocolate?" Delhia asked.

Tina was about to respond but she quickly hung up when she saw Delhia's limo pull up at Miquel's house.

"Why you hang up? " Vanilla asked Tina.

Tina pointed to the limo and responded, "That's her."

The girls watched as Miquel jumped out of the limo and went inside his house. The limo then pulled off.

"Let's follow her!" Said Vanilla and they trailed the limo to Delhia's hotel, but nobody got out of the limo except the driver.

"She's in her room I" Said Tina.

"Well, at least we know that the bitch is in town and where she is stay-ing." Said Chocolate.

The girls pulled off from the hotel and headed to Vanilla's aunty's house to learn everything they were gonna need to know about pushing cocaine.

◆ ◆ ◆

Being hung up on didn't sit too well with Delhia so she called Steve. She told him to get dressed because they were going out. Delhia figured they would go by the "Blue Velvet" to see if they could find Chocolate.

Chapter Eighteen

Miquel was at home getting dressed when he received a call from the police station letting him know that they found his car and he could pick it up at the station. He made it to the station at 9:15 p.m. to get his car and from there he went straight to the "Blue Velvet." On his way to the club, Miquel thought about how he followed Robert to the club the night before. He was glad that he didn't kill Robert. Miquel parked and went inside the club. Once inside the club, Miquel ordered a bottle of Ciroc and then went to the corner of the club where he sat in a booth. He chilled his drink and sipped a bit while he listened to various rap artists blast from the speakers. Several strippers tried to keep him company, but he wasn't interested in any of them. I'm strictly here looking for Tina, Miquel kept telling himself while he fought the urge to get a lap dance.

An hour had went by and Miquel was about to order a second bottle of Cîroc when he saw Delhia and Steve enter the club. The music must've stopped playing when Delhia walked in because everyone had their eyes fixated on her. The sleeveless white leather Chanel cat suit she was wearing showed every curve she had to offer.

◆ ◆ ◆

"Two bottles of Cristal and five-thousand singles if you don't mind." Delhia said to the bartender as soon as she got to the bar.

Delhia knew if she spread a little money in the air, then the thirsty ass strippers would tell on their mamas. So if Chocolate was at work, she wasn't gonna be hard to find. The bartender left the bar and came back handing Delhia two freezer bags of money. All the strippers watched to see what direction Delhia was about to move in. Delhia found a booth in the corner of the club, and on her way she spotted Miquel and she waved at him. He waved back. A s soon as Delhia and Steve sat down three strippers rushed them.

"Have fun with them, Stevie, and ask around for Chocolate. "Delhia told Steve over the music then she sat back and poured herself a glass of champagne.

This was the first time Delhia had been.to a club in years so she decided she was going to enjoy herself. As she sipped her champagne, Delhia looked over at Miquel who seemed to not be paying the stripper at his table any attention. What is his reason for being here? She wondered. After seeing that Steve was occupied with ass and titties playing all around him, Delhia decided to go talk with Miquel.

"You don't seem to be enjoying yourself!" Said Delhia as she sat next to Miquel.

"Nah. I'm here looking for the bitch that stole my money."

"Looks like we are on the same shit, but since we are here, we might as well have some fun!" Said Delhia, then she turned up her glass.

"I' d rather be alone with you." Miquel said smiling.

"Boy, you can't handle this old pussy" Said Delhia twisting her lips.

"Find out!" Miquel told her, then he turned up his bottle. "In due time." Replied Delhia, then she left from Miquel's side and went back to her own booth.

♦ ♦ ♦

By midnight, the Ice Cream Clique had finished their Dope Game 101 class which was taught by Gary Anne, Vanilla's aunty who smoked more dope than many have sold. Gary Anne taught the Clique the rules and the key factors to the game. She also advised them that it was a slight drought and if they could keep up the supply, it damn sure was in demand. With Gary Anne's help the Clique sold everything they had in three hours. Tina did the math and saw that they made $20,000 in profit already. They gave Gary Anne $5,000 for taking them to school. Thanks to aunty the Ice Cream Clique now knew how to weigh, cook, bag, and sell cocaine. Aunty even provided them with a few loyal customers. Now the Clique was ready for whatever, including the niggas who's gonna get on some hatin' shit because the Ice Cream Clique was getting money.

They left aunty's house and went back to the hotel to get ready for the next day. Once they were inside the room, Tina thought she might ruffle Delhia's feathers a little bit. She sent Delhia a text message from Chocolate's phone that read "Nashville Tony with a Gun Emoji." Tina sat hoping that Delhia knew what she was talking about while she waited for a response from Delhia.

After waiting 15 minutes for a response, Tina ended up dosing off.

It was 1:00 a.m. and Delhia still hadn't found out anything she wanted to know. All of the strippers kept telling Steve the same thing, that they haven't seen her since last night. Delhia felt some fishy shit was going on somewhere, but she couldn't put her finger on it. Why did Chocolate hang up on me if she doesn't know who I am? Delhia asked herself. Then she thought about Miquel, who was staked out in his booth drunk as hell looking for Tina. Delhia was tipsy herself and she felt like it was time for her and Steve to leave. She noticed Steve had consumed over his limit of alcohol and couldn't stand up straight. Steve couldn't protect Delhia if he wanted to. Delhia grabbed hold of Steve and guided him out of the club to the limo.

"Get yo ass in! "Delhia told Steve after she opened the door for him.

Miquel came out of the club right behind Delhia to make sure she was straight.

"Ya'll okay?" Miquel walked up behind Delhia who jumped from the sound of Miquel's voice.

"Uh, yeah boy! Damn. You scared me!" Replied Delhia. "Are you ready?" Miquel asked Delhia.

"Yeah boy. Follow us!" She replied.

Miquel got into his car and followed Delhia's limo to the hotel. After assisting Delhia with getting Steve to his room, Miquel and Delhia went to her room. Miquel could tell Delhia was tipsy, so he figured he was about to fuck her, but what he didn't know is that when Delhia gets drunk, she gets on some other shit.

Miquel stripped down to his boxers and laid across the bed. He watched Delhia as she walked back and forth from her suitcase to the bathroom. Delhia got her iPhone out of her purse to check the time, but she noticed that she had a message. That the message was from Chocolate and said "Nashville Tony" with a gun emoji beside it. Delhia's eyes enlarged when she read the message, for one: How does this bitch know that I killed him, and two: This confirms the fishy shit, thought Delhia as she put down her phone and washed the make-up off of her face. After washing her face, Delhia went in the room and put on her night gown.

"I see you got your car back!" Delhia said to Miquel, who was laying on the bed like he was in a Jet magazine centerfold.

"Yeah. The police found it earlier."

"I thought you and Tina were messing around, so why did she steal the car and your money?" Delhia asked Miquel.

"I really don't know. After you and dude left my house, I went and got back in the shower. I was in the shower jacking my dick thinking about you when I heard the exhaust system of my car. I jumped out of the shower and ran to the front door, but she was already pulling off." Explained Miquel.

"She knew you were on some bullshit from the start! Not one time did you open your mouth to say a fucking word while she was telling me about what was going on, but when I leave out of the house you come running with your number offering your assistance. You know what? I like her because she read through you and your bullshit!" Delhia told Miquel.

"So what you saying?" Miquel asked Delhia as he sat up on the bed.

"I would have done the same thing, little boy, that's what I'm saying. " Delhia said wanting to disturb Miquel. So he could leave her presence because he wasn't going to be fucking her anytime soon anyway.

Let me get the fuck up out of here before I knock this old senile bitch out! Thought Miquel to himself as he got dressed without saying a word. Delhia was relieved that her plan had worked, because Miquel was too stupid for her. Intelligence intrigued Delhia's pussy and whoever had text-ed her phone now had her intrigued.

"I'll holler at you later!" Miquel told Delhia as he walked to the door.

"Nah. Don't holla! If I need you, I'll do the hollering!" Said Delhia, then she shut the door and locked it behind Miquel. Delhia sat on the bed and looked at the text in her phone.

She decided to text back.

♦ ♦ ♦

Tina was asleep when the vibration of Chocolate's phone woke her up. After all, she did fall asleep with the phone in her hand. Tina read the message from Delhia which read: "Who is this?" With a smiley face emoji out beside it. Tina wanted to tell Delhia it was her, but she didn't have to because while she stared at the first mess from Delhia, a second mes-sage came through that read: "Tina." with a tongue licking emoji. Tina dropped the phone. She was spooked when she saw her name. Tina got up and went to look through the peep hole to see if anybody was outside their room. She felt like Delhia was watching her. Tina refused to let Delhia think she was scared so she got her own phone and called Delhia.

"Hello?" Delhia answered. "What's up?" Tina asked her.

"I like you. You are a very smart young lady." Delhia told Tina.

"Oh, yeah!"

"Can we talk?" Delhia asked her. "It depends. " Tina responded.

Delhia found herself getting turned on by Tina's voice. "Room 4", at......" Delhia was cut off by Tina.

"The Holiday Inn Express!" Said Tina, then she hung up on Delhia.

Tina grabbed her snug nose 38 revolver and left the room to go meet Delhia. On her way there, Tina thought about all of the possible things that could happen. She just wanted Delhia to leave her clique alone about the death of Robert. Nothing more or less than a simple peace treaty so the Ice Cream Clique can get to the money.

♦ ♦ ♦

Delhia smiled as she thought of how Tina knew what hotel she was staying at. This little bitch got brains and heart, thought Delhia. Fifteen minutes later Tina was knocking on Delhia's door.

"Come in." Said Delhia loud enough for Tina to hear through the door.

Tina walked into the room with her hand inside of her purse clutching her pistol.

"Lock the door behind you, Beautiful." Delhia told Tina, who locked the door and cautiously walked deeper into the room and took a seat in the recliner chair.

"So how do you know about Nashville Tony?" Delhia asked Tina as she got up from under the cover of the bed butt naked and walked to the refrigerator.

Look at this sexy bitch here, thought Tina, as she felt her pussy tingle from the sight of Delhia's sexy body.

"I put all the pieces together that I've heard from everyone and the answer to the equation was you." Tina told Delhia as she gawked at her amazing physique while Delhia stood directly in front of her.

"You're really pretty and smart too." Delhia complimented Tina, then ran her fingers through Tina's hair.

Tina felt her pussy throb and moisten.

"Yeah. But what's up, you still wanna kill my home girl?" Tina asked Delhia, trying not to forget the reason she came here.

"I take it that you've already told her that I was looking for her." Said Delhia as she continued to turn her fingers in Tina's hair.

"She's like my sister, so what do you expect? To keep it real with you, Delhia, Robert really got on some other shit." Pleaded Tina.

"I know, I know!" Said Delhia then she walked off, sat on the bed and started crying.

Delhia finally broke down and let go of some of the emotions that she had been holding in for decades. Tina went to her side and consoled her.

"Let it out, baby. Let it all go! "Tina told Delhia then she took Delhia in her arms and began rocking her like she was a baby. "Thank you, Beautiful." Said Delhia as she raised her head from Tina's chest.

"You I re welcome, Beautiful! " But how did you know it was me?" "You stole Miguel's car and money, plus you are the only person who knew Chocolate to tell her about me. She didn't know my voice to hang up on me." Delhia explained while Tina got her some Kleenex to blow her nose.

"Here!" Said Tina, handing Delhia the tissue.

Tina stared at Delhia while she blew her nose. Damn, this one gorgeous bitch, thought Tina. Then something caught her attention. Tina saw a dildo laying between the covers of the bed where Delhia was laying when she first came into the bedroom. Tina finally gave in and started undressing. Delhia knew exactly what time it was when she watched Tina grab the two-headed dildo and began sucking on it. Tina laid in the bed on her back as she continued to suck on the dildo. Then she spread her legs apart showing Delhia her treasure box. Yes lord, thought Delhia, ready to feast upon Tina's pretty pussy. Tina took the dildo from her mouth and entered the part she had in her mouth into her pussy.

"Oooohha ahhhhhhh!" Cooed Tina as she entered the dildo inside her wetness.

Delhia took the other end of the dildo into her mouth and lubricated the head of it with her saliva. Then she took the dildo out of her mouth and positioned her body perpendicular to Tina's body so that the both of them could enjoy the dildo while they explored each other's bodies with their hands. Before either lady could blink their eye, the two red bone lovers were locked up like crabs.

After an hour of passionate orgasmic lesbian sex, Tina and Delhia were both exhausted from producing multiple orgasms. Tina was feeling some type of way about Delhia, but she refused to put her heart out in the open.

"Tina!" Said Delhia as they laid next to each other.

"What's up?" Tina replied, trying not to show any emotion.

"I love you." Delhia told her.

Those were the words that Tina wanted to hear, but they were also the words she was afraid of as well.

"Don't play with me, Delhia!" Said Tina. Then she jumped out of the bed and started grabbing her clothes.

Delhia jumped out of the bed right behind Tina, who had started crying as she gathered her belongings.

"Baby, please don't leave me." Delhia grabbed Tina's arm. Tina stopped moving and looked into Delhia's eyes.

"Delhia, don't play with me. I'm getting tired of getting hurt." "Baby, I'm too old to play. I'm giving you all of me in return for all of you. "I'm yours!" Delhia told Tina and they hugged and kissed one another.

"Since you're mine, I guess I gotta take care of your little problem for you." Tina told Delhia.

"But I thought she was like your sister! " Delhia thought Tina was talking about Chocolate.

"No. I'm talking about Nashville Tony's son." Tina observed the change in Delhia's facial expression.

Tina could tell that Delhia was lost. "Miquel." Said Tina.

"I thought I was trippin'. Delhia was not believing the shit she had just heard from Tina.

"Don't worry, baby. We'll handle him later. Bet's get some rest." Trina told Delhia and then they went to sleep in each other's arms.

Chapter Nineteen

Greg was awakened by the smell of cheesy eggs, beef sausage, grits and biscuits. By the time he opened his eyes, Nicole was sitting a tray of food across his lap.

"Thanks, baby. It sure smells good!" Greg told Nicole, then he reached over and kissed her.

"I gotta feed daddy, don't I?" Nicole kissed Greg back. If you were a fly on the wall you would've thought that Nicole and Greg had been together for years by the way they acted with one another. They ate breakfast and watched the news. The news aired Robert's murder again. Greg looked to Nicole to emote but she didn't. It was like Nicole didn't know who Robert was.

"I see somebody is heartless." Said Greg.

"Nah. I'm just over the hurt! I mean he was really asking for what happened to him."

"When a woman is fed up, it's nothing you can do about it." Greg sang out loud, then he and Nicole burst into laughter.

"So baby, what you wanna do today?" Greg asked Nicole.

"I don't know" baby. Let's go fishing! "Said Nicole after she thought about it.

Greg and Nicole finished their breakfast and then they geared up to go fishing. Greg felt like the luckiest man in the world to be with Nicole, who was feeling the same way about him.

Nicole felt safe with Greg. Every time their eyes met each other's' they smiled. It was the real thing that they both were feeling.

◆ ◆ ◆

Vanilla and Chocolate had been up since around 6:00 a.m. trying to get in touch with Tina. When Chocolate first got up and saw that Tina was gone, she looked through her phone and noticed that Tina and Delhia had been texting while she and Vanilla were asleep.

"Do you think Tina is trying to set us up?" Chocolate asked Vanilla, who was busy counting money they had made the night before.

"I don't know what is going on, but we're about to dip. Put everything in the suitcase. I am about to call us a cab. Vanilla told Chocolate who was acting paranoid.

The cab arrived twenty minutes later to pick them up from the room. As soon as they got inside the cab, Chocolate's phone rang and it was Delhia's number.

"Oh shit, Vanilla. That bitch's number is calling me back" Chocolate said not knowing what to do.

"Give me the phone bitch." Vanilla snatched the phone away from Chocolate.

"YEAH!" Vanilla screamed into the phone.

"What's up, sis?" Tina laughed at how Vanilla answered the phone.

"Fuck you mean what up bitch? You trying to set us up is what's up!" Vanilla yelled into the phone, not finding shit funny.

"Sis, chill Boo. Ain't no beef!" I'm with Delhia and she's my woman!"

"Oh bitch. You crazy! Where you at?" Vanilla asked, losing her attitude.

"I'm at the Holiday Inn Express downtown. Come get your car. Plus my baby wanna meet you all."

"Bet. We are in a cab right now on the way." Replied Vanilla. and they hung up the phones.

"What she say?" Asked Chocolate's scary ass.

"She said her and her ol girl together now, but strap up because we about to find out!"

Ten minutes later, they were knocking on Delhia's room door ready to go in blasting, but when they stepped inside the room they saw that Tina was telling the truth. Tina and Delhia were acting like two love birds. But when Chocolate laid eyes on the dildo sitting on the night stand that put the cake on the table with all the icing, too. Delhia told her clique how she supported their plans of taking over the dope game. She let them know how she had connections on every type of drug and if they were seriously ready to take over, she could help them. The clique told Delhia that they were ready. The women ate breakfast as they brainstormed their ideas. Afterwards, the Ice Cream Clique compromised on a master plan. Tina told Vanilla and Chocolate to take the money that they made last night and go shopping because once they started grinding, playtime was over. Vanilla and Chocolate were more than happy to leave Tina at the room with Delhia.

◆ ◆ ◆

Miquel woke up around "11:00 a.m. with a slight hangover from the night before. His mind immediately raced to where he could find Tina. He checked his phone but he had no missed calls. How did I just have bitches leaving their husbands and fighting over me to having no bitches at all? Miquel asked himself, but he couldn't come up with an answer. He got tired of wrestling with the thoughts and decided to go for a ride to get some fresh air. As he rode around the city Delhia crossed his mind so he called her phone, but didn't get an answer.

He decided to ride by the hotel since he wasn't going anywhere special and had nothing to do. When he pulled up at the hotel and saw Delhia's limo, he knew she was there. As he got out of the car, he called Delhia's phone again. While he listened to the phone ring, Miquel looked towards the entrance of the hotel. He damn near fainted when he saw Delhia, Tina, and Steve walking out of the hotel and get into the limo. What the fuck is really going on? Miquel said to himself as he found himself dumbfounded at what he was seeing. He quickly jumped back into his car before they could notice him. These bitches actually walking together and holding hands, thought Miquel. He wanted the limo to get long gone before he left the hotel's parking lot.

On his way home, Miquel started to feel like his life might be in danger. Shit just wasn't adding up in his mind. The sad part about it was he was absolutely right. Steve saw him when he first pulled into the hotel parking lot. Steve was standing by the front door of the hotel lobby waiting for

Delhia and Tina when he saw Miquel pull into the parking lot. Steve got in the limo with Delhia and Tina, but he got dropped off at the rental car that they had parked behind the hotel and he was now trailing Miquel.

Miquel pulled into his driveway and a new model Chevy similar to the loaner car he had the other day pulled up behind him.

Miquel got out of his car and walked to the Chevy to see who it was. As he looked inside the car, he could tell that it was a man inside the car with his head down. The window of the Chevy came down and Steve raised up with a desert eagle and a silencer attached to it. Miquel was struck frozen in place.

---POP, POP---

Steve hit Miquel twice in the chest.

"Aghhhhh!" Grunted Miquel as he fell to the ground.

Steve reversed out of the driveway and smashed off, peeling rubber while Miquel laid in his own front yard with his body burning from the bullets he received. The neighbors ran outside to see what was going on when they heard the squealing from Steve driving off.

Chapter Twenty

"Come on baby! You can do it!" Greg cheered on Nicole. "Ehhmm, ehhmm! " Nicole screamed as she pushed as hard as she could to deliver the baby.

"Come on, Mrs. Preston. Give me one good push and give it your all." Dr. Blaylock instructed Nicole while she pushed once more.

"Whiii, whiii, whiii!" The baby was delivered. "Congratulations! It's a boy!" Said Dr.

Blaylock as he handed' Greg the scissors to cut the babies umbilical cord. Nicole watched Greg as he cut the cord while she tried to calm her breathing. After he cut the cord, Greg held his son, but to his amusement, he didn't feel any special connection or bond between himself and the child.

KNOCK   KNOCK   KNOCK

Greg was brought out of his thoughts by the sound of the knocking on his office door. He looked at the surveillance monitor and saw that it was an employee so he pushed the button on his desk to open the office door.

"Hi, Mr. G. I just wanted to pay my tip-out before I got dressed." Sensation walked into Greg's office wearing a pair of black tights, which exposed her camel toe with a halter top and a pair of number eleven Michael Jordan sneakers. The thick, curvy body of sensation was enough to make any man lust. She handed Greg a hundred dollar bill and waited for him to say something, but he never said anything. He just continued to puff on his Cuban cigar.

Sensation saw that her boss was not in the mood for conversation, so she left out of his office. Normally, Greg would've held a short conversation with her, but tonight was different.

Once the door shut behind Sensation, Greg's attention flowed back to the sheet of paper he was holding in his hand. It was the paternity test that read that Gregory Preston was excluded from being the-father of Jaden Preston due to an insufficient amount of matching alleles.

Two weeks ago when Nicole and the baby made it home from the hospital, Greg took it upon himself to find out why he didn't feel as if the baby was his. As soon as Nicole took her first shower at home from being at the hospital, Greg swabbed the baby's mouth with a Q-tip. The next day Greg sent the paternity test off to the lab and had the results mailed to his club.

Now sitting in his plush office at OG's, short for Original Gentleman, Greg grew angrier and angrier as he looked at the paternity test. He couldn't believe how Nicole had betrayed him by trying to put a child on him that wasn't his. Greg threw the sheet of paper then slapped the picture of Nicole and the baby off of his cherry wood office desk.

Greg poured himself another shot of Don Julio and leaned back in his mahogany leather recliner while he puffed on a Cuban cigar. Upon getting married to Nicole, Greg had promised himself that he wouldn't return to his old player ways, but bitches aren't loyal.

Greg knew Nicole was still seeing Miquel, but she didn't know how he knew. Greg was too busy building a solid foundation for his empire with Nicole's money to let something so petty as some pussy get in the way. Now that he was a made man, it was time to cut the bitch off who let him talk to a baby inside her stomach for nine months that wasn't his.

Chapter Twenty-One

At nine o'clock in the morning, Delhia stood in the patio door of her five bedroom, six bathroom mini-mansion, sipping on a glass of wine while she watched Brian, the landscaper work on her backyard. The house was delightful to Delhia, especially since she gamed Tina into buying it and putting it into her name. Tina's name wasn't on anything.

Delhia had hired Brian a week ago when he knocked on her front door passing out flyers and business cards. He had a photo log of his work and Delhia liked what she saw. Now he was in her back yard digging up soil wearing a wife beater and a pair of jeans. Delhia admired his 6 foot, 2 inch, 205 pound frame which was coated with chocolate brown skin. Every time Brian shoveled the dirt, Delhia could see the definition of his muscular arms. She ran her tongue around the rim of the glass of wine she was drinking as she thought about licking the sweat off of Brian.

Brian stopped shoveling and wiped his face with the wife beater, revealing his six pack of abs. When he let his shirt down, he looked towards the house and saw Delhia standing in the patio door smiling and waving at him flirtatiously, so he waved back.

Girl stop before you get yourself in trouble. Nah, fuck that.

I'm tired of my bitch anyway. Delhia conversed with herself. Unable to fight the request coming from her vagina, she stuck her hand inside the tights she was wearing and began massaging her clit.

"Oohh shitt," moaned Delhia as she imagined it was Brian running his tongue across her little man inside the boat. Since her pussy was as wet as a splash pad, she penetrated two fingers inside and stroked her pussy walls with satisfaction. Delhia took her hand out of her tights and tasted her own juices. After she licked the sweetness from her fingertips, she stuck her hand back inside of her tights, sticking two fingers back into her extremely hot volcano, which was about to erupt. As soon as she was about to climax, Delhia was interrupted by the sound of the garage door opening. Damn, thought Delhia as she walked to the kitchen sink to wash her hands.

Brian stood in disappointment as he watched Delhia walk away from the patio door. He took another swig of his water and went back to work.

Delhia dried her hands and plopped down onto the couch acting as if she had been watching TV. A minute later Tina walked into the den area and sat her baby next to Delhia on the couch. Delhia quickly grabbed CJ out of his car seat.

"What mama baby doing? "Delhia held CJ in the air playing with him. Tina sat down beside them and began looking for something on her phone that she wanted to show Delhia.

"What did the doctor say?"

"He gave CJ his check up and scheduled us to come next month for his shots. Oh yeah. He asked me why I wasn't listed as CJ's legal guardian anymore. Look at this." Tina handed Delhia her phone.

Delhia looked at Tina's phone and saw the Instagram pictures of Chocolate and Vanilla with bandanas tied around their faces, sitting at a round table with stacks of money and guns on top of the table. The post on the picture read "Ice Cream Bitches Forever." Delhia shook her head in disbelief at how stupid they were and she tossed Tina's phone back to her.

"I told ya'll that Instagram and snapchat shit is gonna get ya'll fucked up! Ya'll some dumb ass bitches!" Delhia dogged them out to Tina's face.

Tina didn't think anything was wrong with the pictures. She was showing Delhia the office they had bought, but Delhia jumped on some whole other shit.

"I see you didn't pay any attention to the office we bought."

"No. And I don't give a fuck about it. I plugged ya'll hoes in with my Cuban connection and ya'll hoes just said fuck me cause I never received a dime from you bitches." Delhia was mad as fuck.

"Whiii, whiii, whiii.CJ started crying and Tina reached for him.

SLAP!

Delhia slapped Tina's hand away from the baby.

"Bitch, you better get back. This is my damn baby. Or did you forget?" Delhia screamed at Tina, ready to lay the baby down and get in her shit.

"I ain't got time for your shit, Delhia." Tina knew that Delhia was dead ass serious, so she got up from the couch, grabbed her purse and left out of the house.

♦ ♦ ♦

Tina got inside of her white Porsche Panamera that sat on twenty-two inch Forgiatos and left the house going to Vanilla's house. While she drove, Tina couldn't help but to think of-how Delhia had been acting so possessive over CJ. When Tina and Delhia found out Tina was pregnant, Tin didn't want the baby, but Delhia insisted that she had the baby and give her custody. Since the day CJ was born, Delhia hadn't paid any attention to Tina. Tina knew that Delhia had got what she wanted from her and now she didn't want her anymore.

"I still love, I still love, I still love, I still love"

Nicki Minaj blasted from the speakers, causing Tina to get deeper into her feelings and start crying. She knew the love that she and Delhia once shared was now dead.

Tina pulled into Vanilla's driveway at 10:00 a.m. She pulled herself together, dried her face, then got out of the car and rang the doorbell.

"Come in." Shouted Vanilla while she laid on her white leather sectional texting her secret lover.

Tina entered the house and went to sit beside Vanilla. She tried to cease her tears but once she sat down they overpowered her. Vanilla was in the middle of texting when she heard Tina sniffing. Vanilla sat up on the couch.

"Bitch, what's wrong with you?" Vanilla was concerned as to why Tina was crying, but Tina didn't respond. She just covered her face.

"Sis, you betta talk to me!" Vanilla jumped off the couch and stood in front of Tina.

"It's over with between me and Delhia, "said Tina and Vanilla looked at her like she was crazy.

"Forreal Bitch" Vanilla couldn't believe Tina was crying over Delhia.

"Yes, bitch. Forreal!" Tina didn't catch Vanilla's sarcasm.

"Nah, bitch. Forreal you sittin here cryin over that old ass bitch!" Vanilla threw her hands up and turned around in a circle.

"Vanilla, don't do that!" said Tina as she wiped the tears from her face.

"Nah bitch, you don't do that! We gettin money and evidently you don't know what money do, so let me show you. ERIC!" Screamed Vanilla, while Tina looked confused to what she was trying to demonstrate until Eric, a tall light-skinned dude came downstairs into their presence.

"What's up, baby?" Eric asked Vanilla who then placed her foot on the table sitting in front of the couch and gapped her legs open.

"Eat ya breakfast," Vanilla demanded Eric and Tina watched dude get down on his knees, pull Vanilla's boy shorts to the side and start eating her pussy. Tina couldn't help but to laugh.

Vanilla then pushed Eric away from her.

"Get the fuck back and go back upstairs to wait on Mama," Vanilla flexed on Eric and he did as he was told. Tina was laughing in full roar now, holding her stomach.

"Bitch, you stupid."

"No, bitch. You stupid. Coming over here crying bout that ancient ass hoe when these niggas out chere serving bitches like maids!" Vanilla kept one hand on her hip while she pointed at Tina with the other one.

"You right, sis." Tina was in a better mood.

"I know I'm right! I never liked ya old hoe in the-first place!"

"Ha ha ha. I know sis," Tina was still laughing.

"Then to put you up on game, every time I meet with Sammie guess who he's talking about" You, bitch!" Vanilla informed Tina needing for her to bite the bait.

"Nooo, bitch!" Tina was in shock that Sammie was asking about her when he knew she had belonged to Delhia. "Bitch, you lying."

"Is pig pussy pork, bitch?" Vanilla fired up her blunt.

"Of course, bitch." Tina smiled.

"I thought so!" Mission accomplished, thought Vanilla as she pulled from her blunt.

◆ ◆ ◆

Nicole held Jaden in her arms while she fed him, but her eyes were focused on the lipstick prints on Greg's shirt he was wearing. Not to mention when Nicole woke up at 6 a.m. to feed Jaden, Greg hadn't made it home. To top it off, Greg was sleeping on the couch, fully clothed, instead of in the bed with Nicole.

Nicole finished feeding Jaden, burped him and put him to sleep. After she put Jaden in the bed she returned to the den area where Greg was sleeping. She picked his phone up from beside him and went into the living room of their four bedroom, five bathroom home on the outskirts of Nashville in a small town called Hendersonville. She unlocked his phone and went through his messages but she didn't find anything that would be of evidence that Greg was cheating on her. She even opened a new message that Greg hadn't opened from someone named Sammie saying that he needed to have a meeting at Greg's club. Nicole didn't have a clue to who the person was, so she locked the phone and placed it back where she got it from.

Nicole thought that she may just be paranoid from her own dirt. Besides, she had been creeping around on Greg on the lonely nights when he was at the club. She knew if Greg found out who she had been seeing, he would surely kill both of them.

Thirty minutes later, Greg was awaken by the vibration of his phone.

"Hello." Greg sounded sleepy.

"What's up, G. I texted you but you didn't reply so I thought I would call." Explained Sammie.

"Yeah. I was asleep, but what's up?"

"I need to have a meeting with my people and Mandy told me to call you to see if I could do it at your place, tonight."

"Yeah, that's cool. I'll be up there at 10." "Bet." said Sammie and they hung up.

Greg then checked his messages and he saw the message from Sammie had already been opened. This bitch done been going through my phone, Greg thought to himself as he sat on the couch. Seconds later Nicole walked into the den where Greg was at.

"Why the fuck you been going through my phone?" Greg was mad.

"The same reason you have lipstick on your shirt." Nicole shot back causing Greg to instantly start looking at his shirt. "I ain't gotta explain shit to you." Greg got up from the couch.

"So you aren't gonna explain the lipstick?" Nicole got mad when Greg didn't respond and he kept walking into the bedroom. Nicole followed behind him. Greg took off his clothes and went into the bathroom. Greg got into the shower leaving Nicole looking stupid.

Nicole slid the shower door open.

"Greg!" She screamed at the top of her lungs, but Greg paid her no attention. She grew frustrated and went to sit on the bed. Why, why, why? She kept asking herself.

Minutes later Greg walked into the bedroom naked, drying off.

"So, you're not gonna talk to me?" Nicole whimpered, but it only fell on deaf ears as she watched Greg walk into his walk-in closet and begin selecting his attire. Not being able to take the silent treatment any longer, Nicole rushed into the closet and got in Greg's face.

"You fucking around on me, aren't you?" Nicole was invading Greg's space but he remained silent.

SMACK!

Nicole slapped the shit out of Greg, but he still paid her no attention and walked past her to the bedroom to get dressed.

"Why are you doing me like this?" Nicole was now crying a river.

"Whiii whiii Whiii," the baby started crying.

"You woke up your baby." Greg finally spoke as he stood up from the bed buckling his belt.

"What the fuck you mean, my baby?! We had this child together." Nicole yelled through her tears as she went to pick up Jaden.

Now fully dressed, Greg walked to the den and grabbed his keys and cell phone off of the couch. Then he thought about the paternity test. He took it out of his blazer pocket, opened it, and sat it on the couch where he was sure Nicole would see it.

"Just talk to me!" Nicole came in the den holding Jaden, begging, but it was too late because Greg was on his way out of the door.

"Shhh. Momma sorry. It's gonna be okay!" Nicole sang to Jaden while she listened to Greg pull out of the garage. She sat on the couch and rocked Jaden. Then she noticed a sheet of paper next to her. She grabbed it and read it.

"Oh my God, NOOOOO!"

Chapter Twenty-Two

ZRRROOM!

Chocolate sped down I-65 headed to Pulaski, Tennessee in her new Maserati coupe. She had a sell for two bricks of cocaine, in which she had in a compartment behind her back seats. The speed limit was 70 mph, but Chocolate was going 95 mph and wasn't because she had a heavy foot. She was super high on Molly and she was feeling like Super Woman. The navigation system read that she was six miles from her destination, so she called her play.

"Aye, where you at?"

"I'm already here at Cracker Barrel." Said Ryan the guy buying the cocaine, whom Chocolate had met at the club two weeks ago.

"Bet. I'm pulling up in two minutes."

"That's my best friend, that's my best friend, that's my best friend." Young Thug blasted from the stereo while Chocolate bounced from side to side with her Glock 40 laying on her lap.

Chocolate got off on Exit Two and traveled a quarter mile to Cracker Barrel; She turned into the parking lot and saw the blue Silverado truck sittin' on thirty-two inch rims that Ryan was driving the night she met him at the club. Chocolate parked beside his truck. Ryan got out of the truck looking dope boy fresh in a Robins outfit and number nine Michael Jorden sneakers. He got in the car with Chocolate.

"What it do, Chocolate?" Said Ryan, flashing his gold grill but Chocolate paid his flirting no mind.

"Not shit. Is that paper together?" She asked him.

"Yep!" Ryan responded as he handed Chocolate a Gucci back pack. She looked inside the bag and the money appeared to be on point.

"Looks good to me. Hold on." Said Chocolate, then she reached to the back seat and pulled a lever which allowed the back seat to come down.

Chocolate reached her secret compartment and retrieved two bricks of cocaine from inside. She turned around and handed Ryan the bricks then handed him a small overnight bag to put them inside.

"Boy, it's a GO!" Said Ryan.

"What that mean?" Chocolate asked Ryan, confused of what he was talking about.

"Freeze! Put your mutherfucking hands up, now!" Screamed Detective Carlson who was standing outside of Chocolate's door with his gun drawn on her.

Chocolate thought she was dreaming. This can't be real, thought Chocolate. She raised her hands in the air. Chocolate was completely surrounded by cops. There is no way out of this, she thought to herself. Carlson opened Chocolate's door and put his gun directly in her face.

"Don't fucking move!" Commanded Carlson and he retrieved Chocolate's gun off of her lap.

As soon as he had the gun in his hand, the other narcotics officers rushed the car, snatched Chocolate out and slammed her onto the ground.

"Ughh!" Chocolate grunted as the Narcs detained her. Once in cuffs, the Narcs yanked Chocolate onto her feet. "Take her to the precinct. " Carlson ordered one of the Narcs and they placed Chocolate in the back of an unmarked car.

Chocolate watched Ryan get out of her car with the bricks and the backpack full of money. The only difference was Ryan now had a badge and a gun on his hip. That nigga was a narcotic the whole time, Chocolate thought in silence as she watched the Narcs celebrate their bust. The unmarked car pulled off from the scene with Chocolate in the back seat handcuffed. Even though it was only a five minute ride to the precinct, it felt like hours as Chocolate's thoughts drifted back to her childhood.

TWELVE YEARS EARLIER

"Mama, where we going?" Ten-year-old Cidney asked her mother Leslie as they got inside the car.

"We're going to meet your biological father." Leslie answered her child as she pulled off from the house.

"But Mama, I thought Rick was my daddy!" Cidney asked Leslie confused about what her mother was talking about. Leslie didn't answer her daughter, she just kept driving, feeling so guilty about raising his daughter, letting her think Rick was her real father. Leslie had been lying to her child for over a decade. Before Leslie got pregnant with Cidney, her boyfriend Rick cheated on her all the time.

One night Leslie paged Rick for hours, but he never called her back. She was at home bored and most of all, tired of being played like a duck by Rick. Leslie decided to page the fine ass dude she had met at the store earlier that day. The guy called her back and they decided to meet up. One thing led to another inside his car at the park and they had sex.

Leslie only wanted to get some get back on Rick for cheating on her, but she ended up getting pregnant that night. She knew it was dude's baby because she and Rick didn't have sex that week, but Rick didn't know that. Hell, he was so caught up with his other women that he didn't bother to show up the day Cidney was born.

Two days after Cidney was born Rick showed up at the hospital with a car seat and baby clothes. He lied to Leslie like he had went to jail, that's why he couldn't make it the day she delivered Cidney. Rick immediately became infuriated when he saw his daughters' last name was Preston. Leslie told Rick she was mad at him for not being there so she gave the baby her father's last name. Rick didn't know Leslie's father so he couldn't prove she was lying, even though he felt there was some bullshit in the air.

Ten years had passed since the birth of Cidney when Leslie ran into her child's real father at the same store they had first met at. Leslie felt like it was fate that they ran into each other while Rick was locked up so she informed the guy about Cidney. The guy was very intrigued and determined to take care of his child.

They agreed to meet at the Opry Mills Mall in the parking lot in front of the Nike Warehouse at 2 p.m. that day.

When Leslie pulled into the mall parking lot in front of the Nike Warehouse she saw the man they were coming to meet in hand cuffs surrounded by police. A tear ran down Leslie's face.

"No, Greg. No!" Cried Leslie as she banged on the steering wheel.

"Mama, who is Greg?" Cidney asked curiously.

Leslie pointed at Greg as he was being put in the police car.

Greg saw Leslie in her car with the little girl pointing at him. Greg and Cidney's eyes locked onto one another.

"Who is he, Mama?" Asked Cidney.

"That's your real father!" Said Leslie as she and Cidney watched Greg get hauled off to jail.

That was the first and last time Chocolate saw her real father.

Chocolate was brought out of her thoughts by the chiming of the police car when the officer opened the door. The officer escorted Chocolate to an interrogation room and un-cuffed her. Chill bumps covered her body as she sat at the table inside the cold room. How this could be happening to roe, Chocolate thought to herself. Detective Carlson entered the room and took a seat across from Chocolate.

"Your drivers license says your name is Cidney Preston, but you go by Chocolate, am I right?" Carlson asked Chocolate.

"Yes sir, you're right!"

"Now you have some ugly charges, young lady, that can land you in prison for a very, very long time." Carlson told her.

"I know sir. Can I please talk to my lawyer?" Chocolate already knowing where the conversation was headed.

"Are you sure you don't wanna help yourself?" Carlson asked Chocolate, surprised at the way she was handling the situation.

"I just wanna talk to my lawyer." Chocolate knew she was better off dead than making a deal with the devil.

"Okay, have it your way! But I must warn you that the Feds will most likely pick up your case. Carlson informed Chocolate, but she remained silent.

Carlson hated the fact that Chocolate wasn't talking. His breathing grew heavy and he became enraged.

"Got damn it! I'm telling you that the mutherfucker you are dealing with ain't worth you spending the rest of your damn life in prison." Carlson said, slamming his fist down on the table, but Chocolate never spoke another word.

♦ ♦ ♦

As Miquel did his last set of pushups on the floor of his one room bed-room apartment in East Nashville, his cell phone kept constantly ringing. Since the day he got out of the hospital from being shot, Miquel had been working out daily, trying to get his strength back after he suffered from losing a substantial amount of blood. He couldn't wait to get his hands around the neck of every one of the motherfuckers that had something to do with him getting shot. Except for Nicole, of course, because she was the first to find out he wasn't dead. She made sure Miquel was straight at all times.

Miquel got up from the floor and turned up his bottle of water, then he went and sat down on the couch. He checked his phone and when he saw all the messages from all of his women, it made him laugh. He vowed to himself to never fall for a woman's bullshit ever again, since that's how he ended up getting shot in the first place.

Miquel started replying to the text messages, but in the middle of a text his phone began to ring.

"Yeah!" He answered.

"Are you busy?" Nicole asked him.

"Nah, what's up?" He replied as he smiled at the thought of how Nicole had been sneaking around calling and occasionally coming to see him when Greg wasn't around. He hadn't even seen Nicole since she had her baby.

"We need to talk!" Said Nicole, wondering what Miquel's response was gonna be.

"Okay, talk!" Responded Miquel being nonchalant.

Nicole hated the way Miquel talked to her but she still chased him every day like a crack-head trying to get that first high again. Seconds went by as Nicole built up her confidence. Here goes nothing, thought Nicole.

"Jaden is your son." Said Nicole, feeling ashamed about the situation and it didn't make it any better when she heard Miquel burst into laughter.

"Ahh, ha!" Laughed Miquel, who found what Nicole was saying to be a joke.

"Bitch, tell that to Greg!" Miquel told Nicole then he hung up on her.

Nicole couldn't believe how Miquel cursed her out and hung up on her. She felt so stupid. Postpartum depression started sinking in on Nicole as she suddenly began wishing she never had Jaden. Nicole threw her phone across the room and started pulling her hair and yelling while she cried uncontrollably. Nicole thought Jaden was the icing on the cake to her marriage, but she was wrong because he only brought turmoil and misery.

Jaden woke up and started crying, which only added kerosene to Nicole's fire. Nicole fell to the floor crying.

"Shut up!" She yelled as though the baby could understand her.

Nicole even had thoughts of going into her bedroom and strangling little Jaden.

"Ding! Dong! Ding! Dong! The doorbell sounded.

"Go away!" Nicole shouted to the top of her lungs.

"Nicole, are you okay? What's going on in there?" Valerie Nicole's mother asked from the other side of the door.

Nicole realized it was her mother and she got up from the floor to open the door.

"Oh, my God! Nicole baby. Are you okay?" Valerie asked Nicole then she darted to Nicole's bedroom to get Jaden, who was crying and wet.

Valerie walked back into the den, rocking the baby in her arms.

"Girl! What the hell done got into you?" She asked Nicole, who was trying to get herself together.

"Nothing Ma." Replied Nicole, wiping her tears.

"You ah damn lie and my got damn grandbaby in there crying cause he hungry and wet." She scolded Nicole.

Nicole couldn't even look at her mother. She just stared off into space. Valerie knew something was wrong and decided she wasn't gonna risk Jaden being alone with Nicole.

◆ ◆ ◆

Chapter Twenty-Three

"Tonight it's going down at club OG's. The first fifty ladies that are beautiful to the owner's eye will get the total VIP package for free. That's right. For free! Dress code will be in full effect. We got something special for the Baller Shot Callers. Brazilians, Cubans, Haitians and some of the baddest women from the islands will be taking the poles tonight. So men, if you ain't gotten grand to blow, please stay at home. Doors open at ten p.m., so be there. "

Greg had just left the radio station paying the DJ a thousand dollars to spin his advertisement for the party he was throwing at OG's. With all the fuckery going on, Greg needed something to ease his mind and tonight's event was gonna be just that. Plus Greg would get to hand pick through the sexiest women from surrounding areas to enter VIP for free.

It was 3 p.m., so Greg figured he had time to go shopping and check into a hotel room. Hell, the way I'm feeling tonight, I might even buy a new whip just to stunt a lil bit, Greg thought to him self. Business had been good for the past six months, ever since the Grand Opening of OG's. Greg was glad he went with his first mind and went on with his plans of opening his club because he would've only wasted time waiting for the baby to arrive. Shit worked out for the best in Greg's mind. He had love for Nicole but her infidelities made her the enemy. Evidently they weren't meant to be, so he wasn't stressin. Greg snapped out of his thought as he pulled into Foreign Luxuries Dealership located on Lebanon Road. Before Greg could park, he had already seen what he was about to purchase.

◆ ◆ ◆

Delhia was laid back soaking in her hot tub when she heard the advertisement about heparty at OG's on the radio. Sounds like I need to be there tonight, Delhia thought to herself as she sipped from her wine glass. She hadn't been to a club in a while since she sent her bodyguard back to Jamaica. Steve, the bodyguard was forced to leave when he fucked up on a mission, leaving Miquel alive. Delhia was upset and highly pissed off when she found out Miquel was still alive. She immediately told Steve to get the fuck away from around her and sent him on the first flight from Nashville to Jamaica. She really didn't have any use for Steve in the states anyway.

Now after being cooped up in the house for damn near a year, Delhia was ready to get her some fresh air and fresh meat. She called and got her a babysitter in route for the night. Then she began thinking about what she was gonna wear. I'm gonna find me a husband tonight, Delhia laughed at her thoughts.

◆ ◆ ◆

"You know you gonna have to pay for that work you got caught with, right?" Vanilla was already buggin Chocolate about the money for the dope and she hadn't been out of jail for five minutes.

"Bitch, I got popped. They took my whip and all you worried about is me paying for some muthafuckin dope!" Chocolate couldn't believe how petty Vanilla was acting, but she had been feeling the slick hating from Vanilla since she was moving more work than her.

"Uhh, yeah bitch! You must want me to throw up the twenty bands we just bailed you out with?" Vanilla was still on the bullshit.

"Ya'll stop!" Tina said, interjecting between Vanilla and Chocolate. She had compassion for Chocolate because she knew how it felt to be busted with drugs.

"Why didn't you tell. I know they asked you too. Tina asked Chocolate.

"Cause I ain't built like that!" Chocolate stared out the car window as she smoked a Newport. A tear fell from her eye.

"Come here, sis." Tina climbed between the seats and hugged Chocolate. Vanilla looked at Tina and Chocolate in the rearview mirror and she began getting in her feelings.

"Ya'll hoes need to stop with all that sentimental ass bullshit!" Vanilla teared up. When Tina and Chocolate let go of each other, they looked at Vanilla, who had tears running down her face and they burst into laughter.

"Fuck ya'll hoes laughing at! Ah bitch get emotional sometimes too hell. If it would've been me, ya'll ass would've been in jail too by the time I got through singing! I would've been scared to death. I ain't ever been to jail." Vanilla said jokingly, but Tina and Chocolate knew exactly what she was saying. Just then Vanilla's phone started ringing.

"This is Sammie calling." Vanilla told them. "What's up, Boss?" Vanilla answered.

"We gonna meet at OG's tonight at eleven and make sure that Tina is with you." Tina heard what Sammie said because Vanilla had her phone on speaker phone.

"Okay, I told you. I got you! She'll be there." Vanilla nudged Tina in her side.

"Okay. See you later." Sammie then hung up.

"Bitch, I told you that he wants you and you crying over that old hoe." Tina heard Vanilla but she wasn't really excited about getting with Sammie.

◆ ◆ ◆

As soon as Sammie hung up with Vanilla, he called his nephew Mandy, the boss of the Collect Cash Cartel.

"Yeah!" Mandy answered the phone.

"I'll be at the spot in an hour." Sammie informed Mandy. "There is a briefcase on the kitchen counter. Make sure you give it to my lady friend and tell her that it's a small token of love from me.

"Okay. I'll call you in the morning. Sammie was speaking dry.

He was tired of taking orders from Mandy.

"Yeah! You do that!" Mandy was tired of Sammie as well.

He didn't know why his aunt wouldn't let him off Sammie. At one time Sammie had held a boss status ranking in the original CCC, Crazy Cuban

Cartel. But around twelve years ago Sammie started to flaunt, which was a mistake. One day a group of gang bangers noticed Sammie's flashiness and they followed Sammie to his stash house. They robbed him for two million in cash and over five million worth of drugs, Sammie's carelessness damn near caused him to get killed. He did get demoted significantly in the CCC, which was ran by his dying uncle Juan Torres.

Juan made his niece, Maria, first in command. She renamed the CCC, Collect Cash Cartel after her husband tried to turn her in to the feds after he caught her in their home, making love to one of the negroes, who she sold kilos of cocaine to. Maria called on Sammie to dismiss her problem, but Sammie refused to help, claiming he had no reason to because the family was treating him like a peasant. Young Mandy was walking through the family house when he heard his aunt crying. He knew that Sammie's bitch ass didn't give a fuck about Maria's situation, so he decided to take care of the situation himself. Mandy couldn't imagine letting the only mother that he had ever known, go to prison for life. Therefore he killed the problem. Maria instantly made him the Boss and let him change the meaning of the CCC. She made Sammie suffer by making him a runner for Mandy.

Now still to this day Sammie was nothing more than a runner for his nephew, Mandy and he hated it. He still tried to put on to the people he dealt with like he was a boss, but deep down inside he knew he wasn't shit. Sammie also knew if he fucked up Mandy was gonna try his damnest to get permission to kill him.

◆ ◆ ◆

Even though Sammie had set up the meeting at OG's to handle business, business wasn't his main objective. He had an infatuation he needed to fulfill. He needed to scratch the itch he had for Tina since he first saw her with Delhia. Plus Sammie hated Delhia because she never gave him the time of day.

Sammie didn't have a clue as to how he was gonna get close to Tina considering the fact that Vanilla always met him to pick up and drop off. Then one day Sammie was running behind on meeting Vanilla and he was also running late on meeting Dante, so he had them both meet him at the same place. When Sammie arrived at the park he was meeting them at, he got out of his car and walked to Dante's car, which was two parking spaces away. Just as he reached for the door handle of Dante's 600 Benz, he noticed some action inside the car. Sammie lowered his head to get a better look inside the car and saw Dante reclined all the way back in the driver seat receiving head from Vanilla. Since Vanilla had something he wanted, Sammie figured he would let Dante catch his nut, so he got back into his car and waited for them to finish.

◆ ◆ ◆

"Look my nigga. These hoes damn near got the city on locks, we gotta get they ass." Eric explained to his partner C-Lo while they played tunk for ten dollars a hand at their trap house.

They were the typical street level hustlas, selling anything from three dollar hits to an eightball.

"I know they getting money nigga. I been doing research on dem hoes." C-Lo told Eric.

Eric didn't know what C-Lo had followed him to Vanilla's house the previous night. C-Lo was using Eric to gather all the information he needed to rob the Ice Cream Clique by himself.

C-Lo hated the fact that Eric got all the women. Eric was a pretty boy and C-Lo was black and ugly. C-Lo knew he was ugly because when he was growing up all the girls would call him names pertaining to him being ugly. C-Lo usually had to pay women for sex. C-Lo was now ready to be a boss no matter what the cost cause he knew when he became a boss all the bitches were gonna be throwing pussy at him.

"You probably been doing your research but nigga I helped ol' girl count two hundred thousand last night." Eric bragged. C-Lo wanted to smile but he acted normal.

"That ain't shit." C-Lo lied. He had already started spending the money in his mind.

"If that ain't nothing then watch what I tell you when the new shipment comes in. We'll see how much I tell you then. "Eric kept running off at the mouth, not knowing he was only setting himself up for failure.

C-Lo acted as if the tunk game was more important than what Eric was talking about and continued to cheat Eric out of his money.

"Man, put up or shut up about them funky ass bitches. You probably ain't got five thousand in your pocket, but sitting here talking bout what you helped that hoe count." C-Lo said trying to pick Eric. Eric pulled a wad of money out of his pocket and held it up.

"Nah, nigga. I gotten." Eric boasted, smiling. But C-Lo held his composure and kept playing cards.

Chapter Twenty-Four

Greg pulled up at OG's at 10 p.m. sharp driving his new black on black Ferrari 458 Italia. He turned the heads of everyone waiting in line for the doors of the club to open. Greg lifted the door then stepped his Versace loafers onto the pavement. He was clad in a white short-sleeved Versace shirt and pants outfit. A half-inch thick, diamond cut Gucci link chain with a diamond flooded cross on it, swung from Greg's neck. He had a diamond pinky ring on both of his pinky fingers, but he didn't have on his wedding band. The plain jane Rolex on his wrist shined like new money as he rubbed his hand over the top of his fresh temp fade, which was filled with enough waves to make a muthafucka sea sick. This was the new Greg. He was legally successful and he flaunted it.

The ladies in line shouted at Greg like he was a star as he walked to the door of OG's. In return for their screams and shouts, he gave them a million dollar smile. Instead of going behind the bulletproof window to take money, Greg pulled out a stool and sat it a few feet behind where the security did the searching at the front door.

"Boss man, are you ready?" Big Hurt, the head of Security asked Greg.

"Let's do it." Greg replied as he grabbed the roll of tickets that he would be handing out individually to the ladies he chose to party in VIP on him tonight. One by one party goers came through security ready to get their ball on. It seemed like all the hustlas and gorgeous women dressed in their finest threads came out to party.

Greg had been holding the door down, ta king money and issuing out tickets for about a ha lf of an hour when he heard the security talking to someone in front of them that he couldn't see.

"What's the hold up, Hurt?" Greg asked, never rising from his stool.

"This lady is refusing to wait in line, Boss." said Hurt. "Send her on through, mane. Ya'll holding everybody else up."

Greg told Hurt while he thumbed through his money.

"Do I pa y you?" The lady asked Greg, whose focus was on the Benjamins he was counting.

"Yes, you" Greg stopped in mid-sentence when he raised his head and saw the most beautiful woman that he'd ever laid eyes on. She was killing shit softly in the Kim Wooo body dress and Louis-Vuitton heels she was wearing. It seemed like time had stopped ticking with Greg because his attention was frozen on the woman's bangin body, which was accommodated by her flawless yellow caramel skin.

"Boss, you all right?" Hurt a sked Greg while he laughed at how Greg was stuck like he had hit a rock.

"Yeah, yeah. I'm good. Matter of fact, Hurt take over right her and handle shit while I get the misses inside." Greg said, never taking his eyes off of the woman.

"Hahaha, all right, Boss. I got you." Hurt replied laughing.

Greg stood up looking straight into the woman's eyes. "Are you with someone?" Greg asked the woman.

"Now I am." She replied.

Then she extended her arm and Greg accepted her invitation by locking her arm into his. Next they walked into the club and went behind the bar.

"What do you want to drink, Beautiful?" Greg asked her over the loud music.

"Wine if you have any." She replied as she looked around the club with admiration.

"I have just what you want in my office." "Lead the way!"

Greg took her hand and they walked through the bar into a hallway that lea d to his office. When they reached his office door, Greg punched in the security code on the keypad and the door automatically opened. Once they were inside the office Greg closed the door and the woman sat down.

"Excuse my rudeness, Beautiful, may I be of the privilege of knowing your name?" Greg asked her.

"Of course, handsome. I'm Delhia. And you?" Said Delhia while she thanked herself inside her mind for coming out.

"I'm Greg and welcome to OG's." Greg leaned down and kissed the back of Delhia 's hand, causing her heart to flutter.

This has to be the finest ma n on earth, Delhia thought as she lusted over Greg.

◆ ◆ ◆

Tina and Vanilla made it to the club at ten till eleven dressed to kill in their matching red and green Gucci Guilty body dresses with red Gucci heels plus the matching clutch purse. They walked straight up to the security and told them they were there for a meeting with the owner. Big Hurt checked with Greg and permitted the girls inside without making, then wait in line. As soon as they entered the club, Vanilla spotted Sammie and his bodyguard at the bar.

Sammie saw Vanilla and Tina walking in his direction and his full attention went to Tina. He had to wipe the drool that formed in the corner of his lips.

"Hello ladies." Said Sammie as he stood from his seat to hug Vanilla and Tina.

"Hi Sammie." They both replied. Then Sammie hugged Vanilla and then he hugged Tina with intimacy.

"I want you so bad, Beautiful." Sammie whispered into Tina's ear while he held her in his arms.

"Stop it, Sammie." Trina said, smiling as she pulled away fake blushing and patted Sammie playfully on the chest. I really don't want you, thought Tina as she started gazing around the club while Sammie pulled out his phone and called Greg.

"Yeah." Greg answered the phone.

"What's up, G? Me and my guest are at the bar." Said Sammie. "Bet. I'm on the way to you now." Said Greg.

"Baby, would you please excuse me for a minute?" Greg asked Delhia.

"Don't take all day, Handsome." Replied Delhia. Then she ran her tongue around the rim of her glass. Greg loved how seductive she was.

"I'll be right back bay." Greg said smiling as he left out of the office, leaving the door open partially. When Greg made it to the bar, he quickly spotted Sammie and walked up to him.

"Sammie." Greg said over the music.

"G. "Said Sammie when he saw Greg and they hugged one another.

Vanilla's full attention was conducted by Greg's appearance when she saw him talking to Sammie.

"Bitch, look at this fine muthafucka here!" Vanilla told Tina whose attention was on how plush the club was.

"Who, bitch? What...." Tina stopped talking when she saw Greg. This was the first time she had seen Greg since the morning Greg and Miquel got into it with one another and Nicole ran off with Greg.

"Watch this bitch." Tina told Vanilla. Then she stepped to Greg and tapped him on the shoulder while he was talking to Sammie.

"Oh shit. Hey, baby girl! How are you?" Said Greg when he turned around and saw Tina. They hugged and after Greg released Tina he turned back to Sammie.

"Ya'll follow me. I know ya'll can't talk in here." Greg told Sammie. Then he led them behind the bar and down to the conference room which was across from his office.

"Bitch, where do you know him from?" Vanilla asked Tina as they walked down the hallway behind Sammie.

"I' ma tell you everything as soon as this lil meeting over wit." Tina told Vanilla.

◆ ◆ ◆

Delhia heard voices coming down the hallway so she got up from her seat to be nosy looking through the opening of the office door. Well ain't this ah bitch, Delhia mumbled to herself when she saw Sammie, Tina and Vanilla going into the room across the hall. Delhia laughed at her thoughts about what she was about to do. She waited long enough for everyone to get settled in their seats then she imperiously entered the conference room and wrapped her arms around Greg's neck.

"Greg baby, where's the ladies room? I gotta pee." Said Delhia while she stared into Greg's eyes, but before he could answer he felt Delhia's hand grip his dick.

"Shit bay. Come on. I'm about to show you where it's at." Greg told her.

"Well, if it ain't my sweet Delhia." Said Sammie, which caused Delhia to look at him in disgust. If looks could kill, Sammie would've been doo-doo dead.

"Boy, I didn't want your sweet ass then and I definitely don't want your sweet ass now." Delhia told Sammie, right before she rolled her eyes at him.

Tina couldn't believe what was going on right before her eyes. She was disembodied by the sight of Delhia all up on Greg. Delhia acted as if Tina was non-existent.

Vanilla saw the hurt in Tina's eyes. I ain't about to let this old bitch shine on my sista like this, thought Vanilla, but just as soon as she was about to say something, Dante and Meko walked into the conference room. Vanilla instantly melted like butter on hot toast.

"What's up, Love?" Said Dante and Meko greeting Greg and then giving him daps and hugs.

"Well, I'm let ya'll handle ya business. I'll be across the hall if ya'll need me. Come on baby." Greg said, then he grabbed Delhia's hand and led her back to his office.

Delhia never looked at Tina one time. She didn't acknowledge her at all. Delhia had treated Tina like she was dead. So many thoughts rushed through Tina's mind that she had to fight her emotions to prevent herself from crying.

"Sis, just chill. I'm gonna handle that bitch." Vanilla leaned over and whispered into Tina's ear, but her eyes were fixated on something else.

Every time Vanilla saw Dante she got hypnotized by his lazy hazel eyes and wanted to lick the tattoos off of his dark brown skin. Damn bay fine as fuck. I swear every time I look at this nigga my pussy starts dripping. Stop looking at him. Ooh, I can't. That bitch got my dick with her. She doesn't deserve him. He know I'm looking at him, too. So you gonna ignore me bay? Don't make me text your phone, thought Vanilla.

◆　◆　◆

"The restroom is back there, baby." Greg closed the office door.

"I never had to use it, I just wanted those lil bitches to see a real boss."

"I take it you know Sammie?"

"He's a nobody. That's why I turned them lil bitches on to him."

"So you know Tina also?" Greg asked Delhia as he laughed at how shit was coming together right in front of him.

"Yeah. We've been together for damn near a year until I called it quits today." Delhia informed Greg who was taking in every word while he poured them both something to drink.

"So you're the infamous Delhia I've heard so much about." Greg said, smiling at Delhia.

Greg's statement made Delhia uncomfortable. She felt like she had put herself in a losing situation. She was weaponless and didn't know Greg to be talking so much. I've been babbling off at the mouth and I don't even know who the fuck this nigga is, Delhia thought to herself and she quickly stood up from the chair she was sitting in.

"I need to go." Delhia told Greg with a hideous look on her face.

"Baby, I'm with you, not against you." Greg assured Delhia when he noticed worry indwell on her face. Then Greg pulled out the drawer from his desk and brought out a loaded 38 special.

"Here baby. If it will make you more comfortable." Greg told Delhia as he handed her the gun. Delhia took the gun, observed it and saw that it was loaded.

"The only muthafucka I give ah fuck about in that room is my niece, Meko." Greg indicated, wanting Delhia to relax.

Delhia thought about the situation and figured she was in good hands with Greg. After all, who would give someone that they wanted dead a loaded pistol?

"I'm sorry, Greg...." She got cut off.

"Bay, there's no need to apologize. I love what I see in you; Sit down, Beautiful. Please relax and talk to daddy.

"This is your house, so make yourself at home." Greg said smiling at Delhia, trying to loosen her up. It must've worked because she laughed, then walked around the desk and sat on Greg's lap.

SMOOCH

Greg kissed Delhia on the cheek as he slid her heel off of her foot.

"I wanna get to know you for myself, not what somebody has told me." Greg told Delhia while he massaged her foot with his strong hands.

"You've got all this going on. What could you possibly want with me?" Delhia asked Greg.

"I want your mind and your heart, Beautiful. The rest is irrelevant."

◆ ◆ ◆

Across the hall inside the conference room, Sammie was trying to get everyone on the same page but Meko wasn't going for the bullshit she was smelling in the air.

"So, Sammie. Let me get this right. You want me and Dante to report to these bitches when we get ready to pick up and drop off?" Meko stood up pointing in Tina and Vanilla's direction. Vanilla knew Tina was intimidated by Meko for what reason she didn't know, so she decided to speak up.

"I ain't gonna be too many more bitches." Said Vanilla standing from her seat pointing at Meko. Vanilla didn't have the slightest idea about who she was fucking with and neither did she know what was about to happen. Meko pulled a Desert Eagle from her purse and pointed it directly at Vanilla's head. Vanilla's eyes damn near popped out of her head when she saw the big ass gun pointed at her skull.

"Bitch, bitch, bitch, now what bitch?!" Meko spat at Vanilla who was terrified.

Baby please save me. Don't let her shoot me. Baby please do something, thought Vanilla as she stood frozen.

"Fuck this shit, bay. Let's go." Said Dante as he stepped in front of Meko and started pushing her towards the door. Dante knew he only had a matter of seconds before Meko started splattering muthafuckas brains everywhere. Meko never took her eyes or gun off of Vanilla while Dante pushed her into the hallway.

Mane, that hoe be trippin. She can't be doing that shit. Meko will kill her stupid ass, thought Dante as he knocked on Greg's office door.

KNOCK   KNOCK   KNOCK

The sound of knocking caused Greg to release his lips from Delhia's. He looked at the surveillance monitor and saw that it was Dante and Meko at the door so he pushed the button for the door to open. When the door opened Greg saw Meko with her gun drawn and he immediately lifted Delhia from his lap. Then he grabbed the .38 off the desk and went to the door.

"What the fuck gain' on?" Greg asked Meko.

"It ain't shit, Unc. That lil bitch over there 'bout to get her ass tamed, that's all." Said Meko.

"Meko baby, sit down." Delhia told Meko as she pulled out a seat for her.

Greg saw that it was only a mild situation between the ladies so he closed the door and went and sat the gun back on his desk.

"Dem hoes don't know who they fuckin' wit, Unc." Meko said, full of cockiness.

"So tell me what went on, baby girl." Said Greg.

"This muthafucka gone tell me and bay that he giving these ice cream whores top spot over us. Talkin, bout when we get ready to pick-up and drop-off we gotta holla at them." Meko told Greg while her heart pumped battle juice through her veins from wanting to deaden somebody.

"Baby girl, don't worry about that. It's nothing." Greg told Meko. Then he walked over to his safe, which was open and pulled out a hundred thousand dollars. He walked over to Meko and handed her the money.

"I want ya'll to shut down." Said Greg.

Dante had his head down until Greg said that. What the fuck this nigga talking bout, shut down, thought Dante.

"But Unc." Said Meko, who stopped talking when she saw Greg shaking his head.

"I'm not asking you. I'm telling you, baby girl. Let shit cool down for a couple of months and then we'll go from there." Greg told Meko, who knew her uncle was a wise man and if he told her to shut down, it was for a good reason.

"Okay, Love. You've got my word." Meko said. Then she stood up and fixed her dress. Next she and Greg gave one another a hug.

"Baby girl, I've got somebody I want you to meet." Greg told Meko when they let loose of their embrace. Then he walked up behind Delhia and put his arms around her neck.

"This is Delhia, your new aunty." Greg said smiling.

While Greg poured everyone drinks and Delhia got acquainted with Meko, Dante was lost in his thoughts thinking about Vanilla. Vanilla had him gone. For the past six months they had texted and talked every chance they got. For the past three months they had been fucking and now feelings and emotions were involved. Dante loved Meko, but he wasn't in love with her. His thoughts were interrupted by the vibration of his phone. He unlocked his phone and checked the message from the number he had saved as Mama in his contacts.

Mama
I LOVE YOU, TAY

◆ ◆ ◆

The conference room had been filled with silence since Meko drew her gun on Vanilla. Tina was thinking about what her next move was gonna be and Vanilla was sitting hoping Dante would text her back.

"So, ladies, are you ready to advance to the next level of the game?" Sammie said, breaking the silence as he stood up from his seat. He walked over to Tina and bent down to whisper in her ear.

"Will you be mine?" He asked Tina, but she didn't respond to his question.

Vanilla was eavesdropping and heard Sammie. She saw how Tina was paying him no attention. Vanilla had promised Sammie that Tina would fuck him tonight and that's why he told Meko and Dante they were gonna have to report to the Ice Cream Clique for pickups and drop offs. Even though Sammie didn't have the authority to make that decision, he made it. He was thinking with his little head, but he prayed with his big head that Mandy didn't find out about it by the time he fucked Tina and put the operation back in order. Vanilla wanted Meko and Dante to have to report to the clique because that would make her the Boss over Dante's bitch. That way she would have more time alone with Dante.

Vanilla reached under the table and pinched Tina's thigh. Tina knew exactly what Vanilla was saying to her. Tina knew she needed to get out of her feelings about Delhia and take advantage of the situation at hand. She could feel Sammie breathing on her neck. In one swift motion she took both Vanilla and Sammie by surprise when she leaned back and met Sammie's lips with hers.

She stuck her tongue in Sammie's mouth and twirled it around a few times. When she pulled her mouth away from Sammies, he was in La La Land ready to play Candy Crush.

"Damn, baby. I'm in love already." Said Sammie as he stood up to regain his balance.

Vanilla poked Tina in her side and mumbled "bout time bitch," under her breath.

"Well, there's no need for us to stay in this room any longer, let's go party." Tina suggested.

"I couldn't have thought of a better idea." Said Sammie and they all left out of the conference room.

When Tina walked into the hallway she heard Delhia's voice on the other side of Greg's office door and she felt left out. Tina really wanted to be in there with the others talking and laughing. Vanilla saw the look on Tina's face when she heard the people talking inside the office.

"Mane, fuck them sis. It's Ice Cream Bitches right here." Vanilla told Tina. Then she handed Tina a gram of Molly.

Vanilla knew once Tina took the molly that her mind wouldn't be on Delhia anymore. Tina opened the bag and poured half of the molly into her mouth. The nasty taste of the drug made Tina make a stank face expression.

"Bitch, let's turn up." Vanilla told Tina as she laughed.

When they made it to the bar, a security bouncer walked up to them.

"Mr. Sammie would you and your company please follow me?" Said the bouncer over the loud music and he lead them towards the front entrance.

When they made it to the front entrance, Sammie, his bodyguard, Tina and Vanilla, all put odd expressions on their faces when they were suddenly surrounded by security. Big Hurt stepped within inches of Sammie's small, five foot five, one hundred fifty pound fragile frame.

"Boss man doesn't want you here anymore, so you must leave." Said Hurt in his heavy baritone voice.

Sammie's bodyguard wanted to step up but he knew he was no match for the six big ass bouncers with guns.

"Oh. Okay. No problem. Come on ladies." Said Sammie knowing exactly what he had done to get such treatment. The security made a narrow path for them to leave.

"Fuck this weak ass club. We can turn up at my house Papi."

Vanilla said loudly as they walked outside. She was crunk from the molly she had consumed and mad that she couldn't have Dante at the same damn time.

"Yeah, we can do that. I'll follow you." Said Sammie, trying to hide how stupid he really felt for thinking with his dick.

◆ ◆ ◆

Eric and C-Lo were standing in line outside of OG's waiting to go inside the club when Eric saw Vanilla walking toward the parking lot.

"Aye baby, where you going?" Eric said loud enough for Vanilla to hear him as he walked towards her.

Vanilla turned to her left and saw Eric walking towards her looking good as fuck in, an all-white True Religion outfit.

"Damn, baby. You looking good enough to eat." Vanilla told Eric, who reached out and took her into his arms.

"I wanna eat you, baby." Eric told Vanilla in her ear just before he let her go.

I can't have my Boo tonight, so I might as well let this lil nigga suck on this pussy, thought Vanilla who was high as hell on the molly and wanted to feel Eric sucking all over her body.

"Well, I'm about to go home and party, so what's up?" She told Eric as she reached and grabbed his crotch.

"My nigga C-Lo wit me. Is that cool?" He asked her.

"Yeah, my girl Chocolate at the house anyway. So come on." She told him. Then she walked away throwing her ass from side to side as she walked to her car. Eric watched her walk away then he went to get C-Lo out of the line.

"Come on my nigga. Change of plans." Eric told C-Lo who looked at him like he was crazy.

"What you talkin' bout fool? You spent twenty five huned on our out-fits and now we ain't goin' in." C-lo said, disappointed that he wasn't about to go in OG's for the first time.

"Nigga, I got you baby boy. We going over Vanilla house and she got a home girl there for you." Eric told C-Lo, who got happier than a mutha-fucka when he found out they were going to Vanilla's house, but he down-played it not wanting Eric to see how excited he was.

"Aight bruh, but this bitch jumping." Said C-Lo acting like he really didn't want to go to Vanilla's house.

Chapter Twenty-Five

Meko and Dante left Greg's office to go home, leaving Greg and Delhia alone. Delhia sat on Greg's lap staring deeply into his eyes.

"What's on your mind, Beautiful?" Greg asked Delhia while he ran his fingers through her silky hair.

"Oh nothing. You just ain't like any other man I've ever met before." She told him.

"Why you say that?" He asked.

"Because. Here you are with a jumping ass club full of gorgeous exotic women, but here you are in your office with me."

"Maybe you intrigue me more than you'll ever know, plus with you I've found a peace of mind tonight." He grabbed Delhia's chin and brought their lips together, giving her a sensual kiss. After the kiss Greg asked her "Would you like to go attend the party with me?"

"Of course, Handsome." She replied. Then she kissed Greg on the lips and stuck her tongue into his mouth. After thirty seconds of passionate kissing, Delhia pulled away when she felt Greg's manhood rising from beneath her.

"I see someone has awakened." Delhia said smiling and they both started laughing. Then they got up to go party.

As they walked down the hallway after they left out of the office, Delhia stopped and looked at Greg.

"Whose party is this anyway?"

"It's mine." Greg chuckled. "What are you celebrating, Boo?"

"I'm officially single. I left my wife today." Said Greg. "Shittn me. I'm right here." Said Delhia and she pushed Greg against the wall then kissed him passionately for what seemed like eternity.

A minute later they entered behind the bar where Greg got five thousand singles and a bottle of Cristal.

♦ ♦ ♦

At 12:31 a.m. Nicole pulled up to the front door of OG's in her silver BMW 750 Li. She got out of the car wearing her hair in a ponytail, dressed in a Dolce & Gabbana halter top with the jeans and sneakers to match. She had no idea about the party.

She had come strictly for answers. Her mind told her that her husband was fucking one of the bitches that works for him and she was about to find out.

"Ma'am, you can't park there." One of the security guys said to Nicole as she walked past him. When she paid him no attention, he got louder.

"Ma'am. I said you can't park there." He said as Nicole made it to the security who was searching for weapons. He ran up behind Nicole but he quickly halted his steps when he saw Big Hurt shake her hand and give her a friendly hug.

"Hi, boss lady." Big Hurt greeted Nicole as he shook her hand and gave her a hug.

"Hey, Hurt." Nicole said, smiling and after they hugged she walked into the club.

Big Hurt immediately called Greg's cell phone, but he got no answer, so he called the office phone where he also got no answer. After he couldn't reach Greg by phone, Big Hurt knew he had to go inside the club to find Greg and warn him that wifey was inside the club. Big Hurt instructed one of the other security guys to watch the door and he took off inside the club to find Greg before Nicole did.

Hurt saw Nicole walking into the crowd of the club, so he ran to Greg's office and banged on the door while he called Greg's cell phone. After Greg didn't answer the door nor his cell phone, Hurt hurried back inside the club to find Greg. He walked through the crowd looking right and left in search of Greg, but he didn't see him. After two more minutes of searching he finally spotted Greg dancing behind the woman from earlier making it rain. There was only one problem, Greg's wife was standing directly behind Greg watching him and Delhia made it thunderstorm on the strippers in front of them.

Nicole walked through the club searching for Greg but it didn't take long for her to find him as he seemed to be having the time of his life with another woman. Tears swelled up in Nicole's eyes as she watched Greg dance behind the woman with his crotch on the lady's ass which she was throwing back into Greg while she drank champagne from the bottle. Nicole couldn't take it anymore and she tapped Greg on the shoulder. Greg turned around, looked Nicole in her eyes and then he turned back around continuing to do what he was doing.

How dare this muthafucka play me like he don't know me, thought Nicole with crushed feelings. Nicole then walked around the front of Greg and Delhia and got in Delhia's space.

Delhia looked at Nicole like she had lost her God given mind. "Can I help you?" Delhia shouted loudly over the music while she tried to figure out where she knew this woman from.

Nicole held up her wedding ring in Delhia's face and looked past Delhia to Greg like Delhia was nobody.

"So this is your bitch, Greg?" Nicole shouted loudly over the music to Greg but he paid her no attention.

Delhia, not being the one to argue, felt very disrespected but she decided to have a passive aggressive attitude about the situation until it dawned on her where she knew the woman's face from. This is the bitch my son was married to, thought Delhia and at that thought she hit Nicole across the head with the bottle of Cristal she had in her hand.

CLOW!

Nicole stumbled back and fell against the stage. Delhia looked back at Greg after Nicole fell and he shrugged his shoulders with a smirk on his face. Big Hurt rushed to Greg and Greg told him to carry Nicole to her car. When Hurt picked Nicole up from the floor she started kicking and screaming, but she was no match for Hurt, who put her in a light bear hug and carried her out of the club. Nicole was so embarrassed that when Hurt let her down she took off running to her car, which was still parked in front of the club and she drove away from the club crying.

Greg called over two waitresses and had one of them clean up the mess while the other one went go get another bottle of champagne. Delhia looked at Greg to see if she could read his mood then she hugged him.

"I'm sorry, baby." She said loud enough for Greg to hear her over the music. Greg pulled away from her and looked into her eyes.

"What are you apologizing for, bay? All you did was handle your business.

Now, where were we?" Said Greg as the waitress handed him a bottle of champagne and two glasses.

Delhia smiled from ear to ear then she reached up and put her arms around Greg's neck, pulling him down to her so she could kiss him.

Chapter Twenty-Six

Everyone pulled up at Vanilla's house right behind one another. Chocolate was laying across the couch watching TV wearing a wife-b eater and a pair of boy shorts exposing almost all of her chocolate curves. When she saw the headlights of a car shine through the blinds, she got up from the couch and opened the front door. She didn't expect for Vanilla and Tina to be back so soon, but when she opened the door they were walking to the door. Chocolate saw two dudes get out of the car that was parked behind Tina's car and then she saw Eric's raggedy Cutlass pull up in front of the house, parking on the curb. Chocolate recognized the first two dudes as Sammie and his bodyguard.

"What ya'll bitches doing back so early?" Chocolate asked Vanilla and Tina as they walked into the house.

"Girl, that bitch ass nigga had the nerve to put us out his punk ass club after Sammie told his niece that we were in charge now. Vanilla informed Chocolate.

"Hell naw, bitch!" Chocolate replied.

"Hell yeah. So we about to turn up here." Said Vanilla as she and Tina started going upstairs.

Sammie walked through the door and the first thing he saw was Chocolate's ass cheeks hanging from the bottom of the boy shorts she was wearing. He was already glad they had left the club. Even though he never told anyone, he wanted to fuck Chocolate just as bad as he wanted to fuck Tina. What Tina and Chocolate didn't know was that Vanilla had already sucked and fucked Sammie months ago. It only happened once because Sammie drowned in the pussy and told Vanilla he knew she was fucking Dante. Sammie told Vanilla he would keep his mouth closed if she hooked him up with Tina and Vanilla agreed. Therefore Sammie and Vanilla acted like they never fucked.

When Sammie saw Tina and Vanilla going up the stairs he reached and grabbed Chocolate's ass while her back was turned.

"Uhh!" Said Chocolate and she turned around to see Sammie's short ass smiling.

"Hi, Chocolate." Said Sammie, then he licked his lips. "What's up?" Chocolate replied dryly. Then she walked to the kitchen not wanting to give Sammie the wrong impression. She knew that Sammie was for Tina.

Sammie and his bodyguard sat on the couch right before Eric and C-Lo walked in the house.

"What up?" Eric spoke to Sammie, but Sammie didn't speak back. C-Lo nodded his head speaking, but he also got ignored. Eric and C-Lo walked to the kitchen and took a seat at the table. When C-Lo saw Chocolate on her tippy toes reaching in the cabinet he hit Eric in the side and mouthed "Who dat?" Eric leaned over and whispered in C-Lo's ear "That's her home girl, nigga." C-Lo nodded his head saying "Hell, yeah!"

"What's up, Choco?" Said Eric getting Chocolate's attention as she was about to come out of the cabinet with two bottles of Don Julio.

"What's up, E? Who dat wit you?" "This my nigga, C-Lo."

Chocolate looked at C-Lo and she couldn't find one thing attractive about him. That nigga ain't even cute in designer fabrics, thought Chocolate.

"Aw, what up?" She spoke dryly.

"What's up, sexy?" C-Lo said with his eyes stuck on Chocolate's nipples that were standing up through her shirt while she gave him and Eric the liquor to pour themselves something to drink.

Sammie was sitting on the couch feeling a little uncomfortable about Eric and C-Lo being there when Vanilla and Tina came back downstairs wearing wife-beaters and boy shorts. Tina walked over and sat in Sammie's lap while Vanilla went to the kitchen to join the others. Sammie's manhood immediately began to stiffen from the feel of Tina's soft ass.

"What do you want to drink, Papi?" Tina asked Sammie.

"I'm fine for now, Beautiful, but I was wondering would you like to go to my hotel with me. I would be more comfortable." Said Sammie, then he nodded his head in the direction of the kitchen.

It took Tina's brain a second to register what he was talking about. Then she thought about Eric and his friend in the kitchen.

"Oh. Okay! That's cool!" said Tina, then she opened the bag of molly she was holding in her hand. She licked her finger and dipped it into the bag then she licked the molly off of her finger.

"What's that, baby?" Sammie asked her, curious about what she was taking.

"It's called molly. It makes your sex drive crazy. Do you want some? "she asked him. Sammie had heard stories about the drug and from what he had heard it really makes the inner freak come out of a person. He thought about the offer for a second.

"Sure. Why not?" He told Tina and she dipped her finger back into the bag. Then she stuck her finger into Sammie's mouth.

The taste of the drug was so nasty that Sammie almost choked. Tina got up from his lap to get him a bottle of water.

"I'm about to leave with Sammie." Tina said as she walked into the kitchen where the others were at drinking liquor and smoking a blunt of gas at the table.

Tina opened the refrigerator and bent over to get a bottle of water. Eric couldn't fight the temptation of looking at Tina's fat round ass, plus he figured Vanilla wasn't paying him any attention anyway. Her ass looks like two pumpkins inside of a pillow case, thought Eric while his eyes were glued to Tina's trick or treat. Vanilla saw how Eric was drooling over Tina and she got heated, but she didn't let it show because everyone might think she was a hater.

"Damn, bitch. You leaving already? Shit, you ready to go chunk that pussy, ain't cha!" Said Vanilla as she got up from her seat and went stood beside Tina.

"Gone make him lose his mind, sis." Chocolate told Tina.

At that moment, Tina turned around facing the refrigerator and started shaking her ass. Vanilla was standing beside her looking at Eric with his mouth wide open as he watched Tina's ass bounce. Tina dropped down to the floor shaking her ass then she twerked it back up and turned around.

"Do you think he can handle that, sis?" Tina said, smiling feeling good from the molly.

"Hell naw!, bitch. That's too much!" Chocolate said, laughing but she wasn't laughing at Tina. She was laughing at how Vanilla was looking at Eric as he nodded his head up and down as if he was saying he could handle Tina. C-Lo also saw how Vanilla was looking at Eric and he started laughing.

"Come on bitch. Walk me to the door." Tina told Vanilla and they walked to the front where Sammie and his bodyguard were at waiting for Tina.

"Can I use your restroom, sexy?" C-Lo asked Chocolate. "Yeah. It's the door right beside the steps by the front door." Chocolate told him, pointing in the direction for him to go.

C-Lo got up from the kitchen table and walked towards the restroom. On his way there, he saw Vanilla standing in the door waving bye to Tina. Damn that ass fat, he thought to himself while he grabbed his dick through his pants. Then he walked into the restroom and closed the door.

Vanilla watched Tina leave with Sammie then she closed and locked the front door.

"I gotta pee." She said to herself and she went to the bathroom. When she opened the bathroom door, her eyes damn near popped out of her head when she saw C-Lo pissing, holding enough dick in his hand to choke a mule. C-Lo turned his head in the direction of the door when he heard it open and he saw Vanilla.

"Damn my bad lil mama." Said C-Lo as he shook his dick to get the last few drops out.

Vanilla didn't say a word. All she knew was she wanted and had to feel how C-Lo's enormous dick felt inside of her. Without any questions in her mind, she was about to find out. She walked inside the bathroom and pushed the door closed behind her. Then she walked over to the toilet and let the seat down so she could sit down. C-Lo never moved. He was still standing in front of the toilet with his dick in his hand. Vanilla sat down on the toilet in front of him and took his seven inches of limp sausage into her mouth. C-Lo couldn't believe what was actually happening to him. Not him, the guy all the girls called ugly man all his life.

Vanilla pushed C-Lo in the stomach, causing him to step back, so she could face off with his hugeness, which was damn near fully erect from his excitement. He had to hold on to the wall beside him to keep his balance while Vanilla stroked his shaft with both of her hands and sucked on the head of his dick. A minute later Vanilla took one hand off his dick and stuck it into her shorts, where she began rubbing on her clitoris.

"Umm slurp, umm slurp" moaned Vanilla while she slabbed on C-Lo's dick that was fully erect reaching ten inches.

Vanilla's pussy was soaking wet and couldn't wait to be penetrated by C-Lo's monster meat stick. She took his dick out of her mouth. Then she stood up from the toilet and took off her shorts. Next she jumped up on, the sink landing on her ass, and spread her legs wide for C-Lo to fuck her. C-Lo was moving too slow for Vanilla so she reached out and grabbed his dick, then slid it into her throbbing pussy. The sight of Vanilla's swollen pink clit had C-Lo's dick harder than Chinese arithmetic as he started stroking inside of Vanilla's wetness. Vanilla searched for something to claw or grab while she took C-Lo's oversized dick inside of her.

"Ahh, shit, ummm" Vanilla moaned getting louder and louder with every inch of hard dick C-Lo drove inside of her. C-Lo suddenly stopped and pulled his pole out of Vanilla.

"Get down and turn around." C-Lo ordered Vanilla.

With her body positioned leaning on the sink, Vanilla reached her hand between her spread legs and grabbed a hold of C-Lo's dick, inserting it into her sloppy, wet pussy.

"Ummm, ummm, shit" said Vanilla as she felt the thickness of C-Lo's dick stretching her pussy walls wider than they've ever been stretched due to C-Lo pushing deep inside of her. Vanilla was a nympho and she was loving every second of her sex session with C-Lo.

"You feel that dick?" C-Lo asked Vanilla and he slapped her on the ass twice.

SMACK   SMACK

"Yes, yes. Fuck me!" Vanilla cried. That was all she had to say for C-Lo to grab her by her hips and start mounting her insides. He was fucking Vanilla so hard that the candle holder fell off the wall.

"Hmm, hmm" cried Vanilla as she started hitting her fist on the sink.

"Where your homeboy at?" Chocolate asked Eric, knowing that C-Lo had done had plenty of time to use the restroom.

"I don't know. Go see." Eric said, trying to be funny as he hit the blunt.

Chocolate got up from the table and walked toward the bathroom.

When she was a few steps from the door she heard the sound of skin smacking and moaning at the same time. She opened the door and got surprised.

"Got damn" Chocolate said out loud from the sight of seeing C-Lo paining Vanilla. C-Lo and Vanilla both looked into the mirror in front of them and saw Chocolate standing behind them. C-Lo stopped in mid-stroke when he saw Chocolate.

"No, don't stop!" vanilla demanded C-Lo and he went back to beating her back out.

"Yes. Right there. Yes!" Vanilla cried.

As chocolate watched C-lo fuck Vanilla, she felt her pussy getting moist from the action that was going on in front of her.

"Ooh ooh ahh. I'm about to cum" said Vanilla as she felt her orgasm coming.

Chocolate's fingers somehow found their way inside of her shorts to her clit and began rubbing on it in circular motion.

"I'm, I'm cummin', ahh, hmm." Vanilla moaned as her body shivered from the pleasure she was experiencing.

C-Lo tried to hold back but when he saw the cream that Vanilla coated his dick with, he couldn't hold back any longer.

"Oh shit, baby. I'm bout to nut!" Said C-Lo with heavy breathing.

As soon as Vanilla heard him say that she quickly moved awkwardly causing his dick to slip out of her. Then she turned around and pushed

166

C-Lo against the wall by the toilet. Next she dropped down to her knees and took his pipe into her mouth.

Chocolate's fingers were now inside of her pussy while she gripped her breast with her other hand. Chocolate was about to bring herself to a climax from watching C-lo and Vanilla.

Vanilla deep-throated C-lo's dick causing herself to gag. Then she pulled his dick out of her mouth and began stroking it with both of her hands.

"Hmmm, hmm, ahh shit!" Yelled C-lo as he exploded, shooting cum all over Vanilla's face.

Eric walked up behind Chocolate.

"What ya'll do... "Eric stopped talking. He looked over Chocolate's shoulder and saw C-lo sweating, breathing heavy with Vanilla on her knees with his dick in her hands.

Vanilla turned around and looked Eric dead in his eyes with her face drenched in cum. Eric was frozen in shock. His legs felt like boiled noodles and his heart was inside of his big toe.

Vanilla didn't make the situation any better when she turned back around and placed C-lo's dick into her mouth, sucking on the head like it was a pacifier. C-lo and Eric's eyes met each other's.

Eric turned around and walked out of the front door. Chocolate felt sorry for Eric so she ran outside behind him.

"E, you can't be mad. Vanilla ain't your girl. Plus she saw how you were drooling over Tina." Chocolate tried to explain when she caught up with Eric, but he just kept walking to his car.

His pride and ego was demolished. Chocolate watched Eric get inside his car and pull off.

When Chocolate went back into the house, C-lo was sitting on the couch butt naked, playing with his limp dick trying to get it hard. Chocolate looked around for Vanilla, but she didn't see her. Chocolate went upstairs and she heard the shower running in Vanilla's bedroom bathroom. When Chocolate walked into the bathroom Vanilla was stepping out of the shower.

"Bitch, you're wild as hell!" Chocolate told Vanilla, who was wrapping a towel around her wet body.

"Girl, fuck Eric. The way he was drooling all over Tina's fat ass. I should've slapped both of they asses.' Said Vanilla, whose statement made Chocolate's eyebrow raise up. Why does Tina have to be a thot and; she wanted to slap her, thought Chocolate.

"It looks like ya boy down stairs trying to get ready for round two." Said Chocolate. Then she snickered.

"Ha. His ass dead. He might as well get dressed so I can drop his ugly ass off." said Vanilla and Chocolate and they burst into laughter.

Vanilla quickly threw on a pair of sweat pants, a t-shirt, and a pair of slides. Then she and Chocolate went down stairs where C-lo was naked on the couch, still playing with his limp dick. Vanilla went and stood in front of C-lo and started shaking her head.

"If I wanted to give you some more of this pussy, you could not even get it. Chocolate, why do niggas with big dicks have problems getting hard?" Said Vanilla and Chocolate then burst into laughter.

C-lo was so shame faced and embarrassed by the way Chocolate was laughing at him. He thought he had earned a spot in Vanilla's life, but he was wrong. She only fucked him to crush his homeboy's feeling.

"Put your clothes on so I can drop you at where ever you going." Vanilla told c-10.

While C-lo put on his clothes, he thought about the way Vanilla had talked to him like he was a bitch ass nigga. He vowed to himself that he would make her pay for the way she had just handled him. Bitch better be glad I ain't strapped now or I would lay her ass down, thought C-lo as he put on his shoes.

♦ ♦ ♦

Chapter Twenty-Seven

After the incident at the club, Nicole drove straight to Miquel's apartment, crying the whole way there. She needed to talk to somebody. She needed to be held and comforted. When Nicole pulled up in front of Miquel's building she sat in her car crying for about ten minutes before she went to his door and rang the doorbell.

Miquel was chilling, laying on the couch in a pair of boxers, watching MTV Jams when he heard his doorbell ring. This can't be nobody but Nicole, thought Miquel as he walked to the door to look into the peep hole. He knew none of his other women had the guts to show up at his crib unannounced. When he looked into the peep hole he saw it was exactly who he thought it was, and he opened the door.

"What, Nicole?" Miquel said with a fake attitude as soon as he opened the door, but he was completely caught off guard when Nicole fell into his arms crying.

She was trying to say something, but she was crying so hard that Miquel couldn't understand one word that came from her mouth.

For some reason when it came to Nicole, Miquel had a soft spot in his heart for her. Therefore when he saw how hysterically she was crying, he immediately became concerned. What the fuck is wrong with her, thought Miquel as he closed the door and flicked on the light switch.

"Nicole calm down." Miquel told her as he held her and rubbed the top of her head.

Miquel lead Nicole to the couch and sat her down. After three more minutes of hard crying, Nicole finally simmered down enough to talk to where Miquel could understand her. She told Miquel about what had happened at the club. He listened to Nicole, but at the same time he was dealing with hate and jealousy issues of his own because Greg had damn near everything Miquel wanted.

Miquel was tired of getting the shit end of the stick. He wanted a big house, a bangin' ass club, and the foreign cars.

Miquel continued to console Nicole while she poured her heart out and apologized to him about the whole baby situation, but he was lost in his own thoughts. This bitch really thinks she can just come over here crying and I forgive her for everything. This bitch got life fucked up. Baby Mamma or not, bitch you about to cash in. And you gonna have to accept shit for what it is cause I ain't cutting none of my hoes off for you. But I'll hit you with this gorilla pimpin tomorrow after you've rested up cause you look like shit right now, Miquel thought to himself. Then he got up from the couch to go fix Nicole a bubble bath.

After Miquel bathed Nicole, he led her to his bed where he dried her off. Next, he laid her across the bed and began lotioning her body while he gave her a massage at the same time. Nicole felt so smoothed and relaxed from Miguel's touch. She felt one hundred percent better than she did when she first arrived at Miguel's apartment. She couldn't believe how nice and caring Miquel was being to her. Miquel had Nicole wishing she would've never left him for Greg. Finished with massaging Nicole, Miquel got up and cut off the light. Then he and Nicole climbed under the bed covers. Nicole cuddled up under Miquel's body.

"I love you, Miquel! I really do."

Miquel let Nicole's words linger in the air for a moment before he said something.

"I've been nothing but a Teddy Bear for you ever since you and Greg first got together. You came around acting like you were so concerned when I got shot, but truth of the matter is I got shot because of your bullshit. You only fucked with me when Greg left you lonely. You had that nigga bustin nuts on my lil nigga's head." Miquel sniffed and took a deep breath.

"I'm gonna be a father to my child, but as far as me and you go, I can't just cut off my lady friends who have been there for me. Just because you tell me you love me doesn't mean you love me, now you get some rest." Said Miquel in a throat cracking voice. Then he rolled over on his side, smiling. He deserved an Oscar for the act he had just put on. Nicole felt so bad about everything she put Miquel through. If she could've seen Miquel's face, she would have known he was some bullshit. I got this bitch just where I want her, thought Miquel as he closed his eyes to go to sleep.

◆ ◆ ◆

Delhia wasn't too enthused about partying for too much longer after the altercation she had with Nicole. So she and Greg left the club to go get something to eat. Greg left Big Hurt in charge of handling OG's for the rest of the night. Ten minutes after they left the club, Greg and Delhia pulled up at the Waffle House. As soon as Greg put his car in park, he noticed a homeless woman sitting near the entrance of the restaurant. He picked up his wedding band from out of the cup holder and gave it to Delhia.

"Give this to her for me." Greg told Delhia.

"Okay baby." She replied and reached over, kissing Greg on the cheek.

They got out of the car and walked towards the entrance of the restaurant. When they reached the homeless lady, Delhia handed the lady Greg's wedding band. The homeless lady smiled from ear to ear, revealing her one big tooth that sat alone in the front of her mouth. "God bless you, you loving couple." The lady told them.

Greg and Delhia entered the Waffle House and seated themselves in a booth. This was the first time that they had seen each other under such radiant light. Delhia took one good look at Greg and before she knew it she was pulling up a picture of CJ on her phone. She studied the resemblance of Greg and the baby.

"What's up, bay? Why you looking at me like that?" Greg asked Delhia, who took her phone and placed it next to his face.

"Didn't you say that you and Tina fooled around when you got out?"

"No. I didn't tell you that, but yes we fooled around once." "Oh my God! Baby Daddy!" Delhia smiled at Greg who seemed to be addled by her words.

"What are you talking about?" He asked her.

Delhia showed Greg the picture of CJ. Greg's eyes loomed and wrinkles spread across his forehead as he looked at the picture of a miniature him. Greg couldn't believe his eyes. Then he took his eyes off the picture and looked at Delhia as a Kool-Aid smile spread across his face.

"Where is he?" He asked her. He was ready to hold his son.

Greg felt in his heart that the little boy he was looking at on the phone was his child.

"At my house with the babysitter, that's my baby, CJ. I made that bitch sign over her parental rights when she had him." She told Greg.

While they ate, Delhia informed Greg on everything that's been going on with her since she came to Nashville for her son's death. Then Greg shared with her all the events of his life from the moment he was released from prison until now. They both found it coincidental that Robert Jr's last day alive was the same day Greg got released from prison. The eventuality of Greg and Delhia's companionship was crazy to the both of them. Greg was eager to hold his son, so as soon as they finished eating they went to Delhia's house.

◆　◆　◆

After Tina sucked and fucked Sammie's tiny Vienna, she took a Xanax and went to sleep leaving Sammie up geeking on the molly. He was the least bit sleepy and Tina's sex didn't do anything for the sex crave he was having. At three in the morning he sat in the darkness of his suite, searching on Backpage for sexual pleasures.

He read a profile listed as Sunshine and she was in the area of town he was located in. Her profile read she was Hispanic and Black, plus she indulged in all types of sexual fantasies. Sammie fell in love with her profile pictures and he called the number on her ad but he didn't get an answer, so he went back to browsing through different profiles.

◆　◆　◆

"Ugh ughh" Sunshine gagged while Eric tried to ram his dick through the back of her throat. He was extremely frustrated from the embarrassment he had endured at Vanilla's house and he was making Sunshine's mouth pay for it. When Eric left Vanilla's house, he came to Sunshine's hotel room where she was at waiting for someone to call her looking for some action. Now receiving oral pleasure from Sunshine, Eric could not concentrate on the good brain he was receiving because the image of Vanilla sucking C-lo's dick kept popping up in his head. Eric said fuck it and took his dick out of Sunshine's mouth, putting it away in his pants.

"What's wrong, Daddy?" Sunshine asked Eric because she really wanted to please him.

"It's nothing," Eric huffed angrily, then he fired up his blunt.

Jada Lewis, a.k.a. Sunshine, has been infatuated with Eric ever since she laid eyes on him over a year ago and she does anything she can to make him happy. She's twenty years old, 5'4" in height, 150 in weight with no stomach, a slim waist and a fat ass. Her bright yellow skin tone earned her the nickname Sunshine. Her green eyes and long curly black hair are products of her half black, half Puerto Rican nationality. Sunshine is a money makin muthafucka. She sells pussy 24/7, 365 days out of the year.

Selling pussy came easy for Sunshine since her mother's boyfriend took her virginity when she was eleven. She has been neglected by every male figure that has ever came into her life. Eric has a million dollar hoe and don't know what to do with her because he's been too focused on Vanilla to concentrate on Sunshine, who only needs a little guidance to get to the top. Sunshine could tell that something was bothering Eric and she didn't wanna make him any madder than he already was, so she let him be and she began checking her phone to see who had called.

"Yes, did someone call Sunshine?" Sunshine spoke in her sexiest voice into her phone. She was hoping that it was somebody who wanted to spend some big money so she could give it to Eric to make him happier.

"Yes, Beautiful. I did. I saw your profile and I'm very interested in you." Said the caller. Sunshine noticed his foreign accent and she put him on speaker phone so Eric could hear him.

"Are you the police or do you have anything to do with law enforcement?" Sunshine asked as a routine question.

"Ha Ha! Well, hell no, Beautiful. In my field of world we do not deal with police" stated the caller, wanting Sunshine to be comfortable with him.

"Well, do you want in-call or out-call?"

"I would like for you to come to me, if that's possible, Beautiful."

"It's three hundred for a half of an hour, five hundred for the full hour and since it's so late my bodyguard must come with me for security purposes. If any of this is a problem, then I can't come." She informed the caller.

"Money is not a problem, baby. I hope your security likes to fuck you because I'm willing to pay ya'll five grand to put on a show for me." Said the caller, feeling hornier than he'd ever felt in his life. Eric and Sunshine looked at each other and smiled.

"Text me your info and I'll be there in thirty minutes." Sunshine thought about the time she and Eric fucked a married couple for a thousand dollars.

"Okay, Beautiful, I'll be waiting." Replied the caller and then they hung up.

◆ ◆ ◆

Sammie hung up his phone and started rambling through Tina's belongings, looking for her molly. He knew she had more and he wanted it. He even tried to wake up Tina, but she didn't budge. After a couple more minutes of searching, Sammie finally found the molly inside the drawer next to the bed. He didn't know how much to take, so he tried to take the same amount Tina had given him earlier. Moments later Sammie began to wonder what type of feeling he would get if he sniffed some cocaine on top of the molly he'd just taken. With over fifty keys of coke inside his suite, Sammie was surely about to find out.

Sammie walked to the closet inside the bathroom of his suite and pulled out one of the duffle bags containing bricks of cocaine inside of it. He unzipped the duffle bag and took out a kilo. He sat the kilo on top of the sink counter. He needed something to carve into the kilo with so he went and got the pocket knife he had in his pants, then he returned to the bathroom. As soon as he punctured the kilo with the knife, a scent was released from inside the wrapper that immediately told Sammie that he had gotten the wrong bags from the stash house. He threw the kilo back into the duffle bag and checked one of the kilos from the other duffle bag, but it was the same stuff as the first one so he threw it back also.

Sammie was about to say "fuck it", but that's when he saw the briefcase that Mandy told him to give to Delhia for his appreciation of the business she has brought him over the years.

Sammie knew better than to do what he was about to do, but the molly was making the decisions at this point. He opened the briefcase. Bingo, thought Sammie when he saw two kilos with a Mercedes Benz sign stamped in the middle of them with fifty thousand in case separating the two kilos. He pulled one of the kilos out and closed the briefcase.

He sat the kilo onto the sink counter and carved into the center of it with the pocket knife. The fish scale cocaine glistened as Sammie broke down the grams he carved out to snort.

SNIFF!!   SNIFF!!

Sammie snorted a long line of the booger sugar and wiped his nose as he lifted his head from the sink. The effects of the cocaine and molly mixed together instantly had Sammie blitzed. Sammie walked to the balcony window of his suite that provided him with a great view of the city and sat down in the recliner chair. The powerful drugs had Sammie feeling bionic.

Chapter Twenty-Eight

At 3:00 a.m. Meko tasted the salty flavor of the tear that had just entered her mouth while she sat on the couch in the darkness of her living room going through Dantes' ICloud. He was in their bedroom asleep, dead to the world. For the past hour Meko had been reloading all of Dante's old text messages and media files from the ICloud of his phone. All types of nude pies and videos of Vanilla playing with her pussy had uploaded back into Dante's phone. There were hundreds of text messages to and from Vanilla. Meko read through many of the messages. She read a few messages that made her smile through her frown. They were from Vanilla telling Dante how they couldn't let Tina find out about them because of the love she has for Meko and the other one was about Vanilla trying to get Tina to fuck Sammie, so Sammie would keep their secret safe. So Sammie knows about Dante fuckin this bitch, thought Meko as she screen shotted the messages and sent them to her phone.

Meko couldn't believe the shit she was seeing and reading. She had been noticed a change in the way Dante had been acting, but she wasn't able to put her finger on the reason why he was acting abnormal. Therefore she decided to go looking for it and I'll be damned if she didn't find it. She was hurt, but she was more disappointed in Dante than anything. Meko felt Dante could've just kept it real and just told her, but instead the only nigga on earth that she had fully trusted with her heart, had played her like a game of Tunk.

It took everything in Meko's power for her not to call Vanilla's phone or better yet go into her bedroom and put a hollow point in Dante's head. She knew if she did either of those two things, she would lose the game and the one thing that Meko was not, was a loser. Damn bay, you started this game so I must finish it, thought Meko as she began erasing everything from Dante's phone that she had uploaded and screen-shotted. When she finished erasing the evidence, she placed his phone back where she got it from and climbed into the bed with Dante to go to sleep. Dante felt Meko when she got into the bed with him. He cuddled behind her, putting his hand between her thighs, getting ready to get Meko's pussy wet, but she cut him short.

"I came on my period, bay," Meko moved his hand from between her legs with a smile spread across her face. You better hope game can recognize game playboy, cause it's on, thought Meko as she closed her eyes to go to sleep.

♦ ♦ ♦

Sammie jumped from the surprising sound of knocking on his room door. He knew he was taking a chance by inviting strangers into his suite without the presence of Nathan, his bodyguard. Fuck it, thought Sammie. He needed some freaky action and a lot of it. Sammie walked to the door naked as the day he was born and looked into the peep hole. Seeing it was the girl from Backpage, he opened the door and welcomed Sunshine and Eric inside. When Sammie and Eric's eyes met, they both pointed at each other.

"Come on in. You're the guy from Vanilla's house," Sammie said to Eric, who was trippin that Vanilla's plug was shopping on Backpage.

"Yeah, that's me! You good?" Eric asked Sammie since he was naked.

"Yes, yes! Close the door, Handsome. Never mind her, she's asleep, plus we'll be in the back. Sammie noticed that Eric was staring at Tina's nude body.

The three of them walked to the back of the suite till they came to the bar by the hot tub. Sunshine had been in many hotels turning tricks, but never had she been in a hotel room that was so big. Eric took a seat at the bar and began to wonder why Sammie called Sunshine when he had Tina's fine ass in his bed, naked.

Sammie turned on Fat Joe and Remy Ma's song "I'm all the way up." Sammie was really feeling himself as he went into the bathroom and snorted another line of coke. After he filled his nostrils, Sammie took ten grand out of the suit, case, walked out of the bathroom and gave Sunshine $2500.

"Well, thank you sir." Sunshine looked at Sammie's small dick figuring this was gonna be the easiest money she ever made. Sammie then turned to Eric and handed him $2500.

"I appreciate it. What's your name again?" Eric was glad that he came with Sunshine.

"Sammie handsome, please call me Sammie." Sammie stepped into the hot tub. Sunshine quickly stripped out of her clothing and stepped into the hot tub. When Sammie saw Sunshine's plump, bald pussy sitting between her thick yellow thighs, he got excited.

"Come on baby. It feels good in here." Sunshine told Eric who stood up from his seat.

"Yeah, let me piss first." Eric walked to the bathroom and as soon as he stepped foot inside he saw an open brick of cocaine sitting on the sink.

"Oh shit!" Eric looked behind himself to see if anyone was watching him.

"Help yourself, handsome. There's plenty where that came from." Yelled Sammie knowing that Eric had seen the cocaine on the sink. Eric felt like a child that got caught with his hands in the cookie jar. He decided not to touch the cocaine and he took a piss.

"Baby, you're beautiful." Sammie eased up behind Sunshine and placed his hands on her hips.

"Thanks, Sammie." Sunshine pushed her ass back into Sammie's pelvis and began rotating her hips.

"I want both of ya'll baby. I'm so horny. Get your boyfriend to fuck me. I have plenty of money and drugs. Make it happen for me baby. Let Sammie take care of you." Sammie moved his hands from Sunshine's breast to her clitoris. Sunshine moved his hand as she turned around to face him. They were the same height so she was looking directly into Sammie's eyes with her game face on.

"You promise that you're gonna take good care of us?"

Sunshine palmed Sammie's balls and began massaging them.

"Yesss, baabyy" Sammie cooed from Sunshine's touch.

Sunshine let go of Sammie and stepped out of the hot tub to go to the bathroom. She knew what Sammie wanted and she knew the only way she was gonna be able to deliver was to get Eric high on the cocaine that she saw Eric staring at when she walked into the bathroom. Eric turned around when he saw Sunshine appear in the mirror.

"What's up, baby'? You straight?" Eric asked Sunshine who walked around him and went straight to the cocaine.

"Yeah, baby I'm good. I just wanna make sure you're straight daddy." Sunshine picked up the rolled up hundred dollar bill so she could snort some of the coke that was already broken down.

"You about to snort some of that, baby?" Eric asked Sunshine with a confused look on his face because he knew how freaky the two of them got when they did cocaine. The last time they snorted some booger sugar together, Eric fucked Sunshine in her ass for hours. Sunshine answered his question without talking when she sniffed a line of coke up each of her nostrils. The cocaine was so potent that when Sunshine raised her head to look at Eric, a tear fell from her eye. She felt an instant drain in her throat.

"I love you, Eric, and I'll do anything to make you happy.

You should know that by now. Here is our chance for you to be on top." Sunshine wiped her nose. Eric was confused about what she was talking about.

"Shine, what are you talking about? He gave us five bands.

That ain't shit." Eric pushed the bathroom door closed.

"I'm talking about more money and big dope. He told me he will give it to us, but he wants both of us. You know he has it. Look at what he snorts out of. You've never had one of these." Sunshine pointed to the brick of cocaine, but Eric had a very confused look on his face.

"What the fuck you mean? He wants both of us, bitch? He ain't about to fuck me!" Eric put his finger in Sunshine's face.

"I know, Eric. He wants you to fuck him." Sunshine stared sincerely into Eric's eyes. She watched as his face muscles relaxed a little bit. She knew Eric was probably contemplating the situation at hand.

Eric knew this could be the opportunity that he'd been waiting on for a lifetime. He had been selling dope for ten years and the most money he ever had was $12,000. Eric had always promised himself that he would never let anything get in the way of him being on the top. He thought back to a couple of months ago when Sunshine asked him if he would suck a dick for a million dollars. When she asked him, he slapped the shit out of her, but now he faced something of that scenario in reality. The only difference was he didn't have to suck a dick, but fuck a man in the ass. Won't nobody know but me and Shine, he thought to himself. Then he grabbed Sunshine by her chin and looked her dead in her eyes.

"We gonna do what we gotta do. Don't nobody love me like you do and I know that, so let's get this money, baby." Eric took the rolled up hundred dollar bill out of Sunshine's hand and sniffed cocaine up both of his nostrils.

He had never consumed so much booger sugar at one time in his life. Eric immediately felt a rush.

"Come on, baby. Let's do this." Eric spoke with seriousness stamped on his face. Sunshine smiled bright as the sun, then she grabbed Eric's hand and led him into the room. When they walked out of the bathroom, Sammie was laid back in the hot tub sipping champagne.

"There goes my two favorite people." Sammie was ready to get his freak on.

Sunshine didn't waste any time. She got inside the hot tub and went straight to Sammie, kissing him on the lips. Eric started stripping out of his clothing. Even though Sunshine was kissing all over Sammie, but Sammie's eyes were locked on Eric. Watching Eric get naked made Sammie's rectum tingle, so he took Sunshine's hand and placed it on his ass, guiding her middle finger to his ass hole. Sunshine followed Sammie's lead and she slowly penetrated her finger inside his ass, giving him great pleasure. Eric then climbed into the hot tub and went straight to work, fucking Sammie from the back while Sammie ate Sunshine's pussy while she spread eagle on the side of the hot tub.

Tina, suffering from cotton mouth, woke up out of her deep sleep needing a drink of water. When she rose up in the bed she noticed movement in the rear of the room containing multiple people. She focused her attention to the action and she realized they were in the hot tub engaging in sex. A light bulb immediately went off in Tina's head. Maybe this is my opportunity to hit Sammie for the bricks he was showing off to me earlier that he put in the bathroom closet, thought Tina as she got out of the bed and put on her clothes. After she got dressed, Tina walked to the back where the others were in the hot tub and she got the surprise of her life. Oh my god! Thought Tina when she saw Eric fuckin Sammie from the back while Sammie ate Sunshine's pussy while she laid on the edge of the hot tub.

Eric saw Tina standing behind Sunshine and stopped fuckin Sammie mid-stroke. Sunshine turned around to see what Eric was looking at and she dumped from Tina's presence.

"Are you gonna tell Vanilla?" Eric was caught, but he didn't want Vanilla to find out no matter how she had fucked and sucked C-lo in front of him. Sunshine got infuriated when she heard Eric say Vanilla's name. She got up from the side of the hot tub and went straight into the bathroom. Tina saw how pretty Sunshine was with her foreign features.

"No, Eric. I wouldn't do that! Now handle your business." Tina gave Eric more motivation. He smiled.

"Thanks! I owe you one."

"Fuck me!" Sammie demanded and Eric went back to work. Tina went into the bathroom where Sunshine was at sitting on the toilet with her face in her hands crying. Tina shut the bathroom door.

"What's your name, pretty lady?" When Sunshine raised her head and saw Tina, she wiped her face.

"Jada. But they call me Sunshine." Damn she's fine, thought Sunshine as she looked at Tina's: curves that were not far from her.

"Well Jada, I'm Trina."

"Nice to meet you and you are also pretty." Said Sunshine while she got herself together.

"Thanks Boo, but why are you in here crying?" Tina asked as Sunshine stood up and blew her nose. She's a cutie, thought Tina.

"Because I do whatever to try to make that nigga happy, but all he cares about is some bitch named Vanilla and I'm tired of it."

Just then a plan popped into Tina's head of how she was gonna take Sammie's dope and Eric's bitch. Tina looked in the bathroom closet and saw the duffle bags that the kilos were inside of.

"Look at me, Jada," Tina said in a sincere tone of voice, causing Sunshine to look her in the eyes.

"Do you wanna leave here with me, a real boss bitch or you wanna stay here with these fags?"

Tina looked more serious than a heart attack letting Sunshine know she was with no bullshit. Sunshine may have been young, but she knew if Eric fucked a man for money, then if it ever came down to him sacrificing her for any cause, he would do it without a doubt in her mind. Plus, Sunshine already knew who Tina was because she was following Tina, Vanilla and Chocolate on Instagram.

"I'm going with you."

"Did you drive?" Asked Tina.

"Yeah, my keys are in my purse on the bar."

"All I need you to do is go distract those faggots. I want you to do whatever you gotta do for me to make it out of this room with these duffle bags." Tina pulled the bags out of the closet and showed Sunshine the kilos. Damn, thought Sunshine.

"I'm gonna be right here looking at you through the crack of the door. When you feel like you got both of those sissys occupied enough for me to leave out of the bathroom, you give me the okay signal then you slip out of the room right behind me.

Don't grab no clothes or nothing. Just act like you about to go lay in the bed. I'll be in the hallway waiting for you." Tina had a helluva game plan.

"Okay. I got you, Boo." Sunshine left out the bathroom to go handle her business feeling good. She went to the couch that was beside the hot tub and she pulled it out of the bed. "Ya'll come over here." Sunshine grabbed the KY from the side of the hot tub while Eric and Sammie got out of the hot tub. She pushed Eric down on the bed and climbed on top of his face.

Sunshine rode Eric's face while she lubed his dick.

"Ooh, yess, come here papi" Sammie did as he was told, and climbed on top of Eric's pelvis area facing Sunshine. Sunshine then grabbed Eric's pole and slid it into Sammie's man hole.

"Ahh yesss," Cooed Sammie as he felt Eric inside of him.

Tina watched Sunshine through the cracked door as she worked her magic. Once Sunshine had Eric eating her pussy and fucking Sammie at the same time, she began tongue kissing Sammie and threw up thumbs up behind his head. Tina knew that was her cue and she came out of the bathroom with a duffle bag on each of her shoulders. She grabbed Sunshine's purse and headed for the entrance of the room. When she reached the door, she looked back at Sunshine and waved for her to come on. Tina left out the door leaving it barely open.

Sunshine stood up from Eric's face and jumped onto the floor. She wanted to make sure neither of the men would see her leave so she pushed Sammie's head down beside Eric's neck.

"Fuck that ass baby." She told Eric and Eric really got into it. Satisfied that she could escape,

Sunshine slapped Sammie on his ass and then began walking towards the room door. She turned around to see if Eric or Sammie was looking in her direction. Neither of them were so she quickly dashed out the door and lightly closed it behind her.

"Come on." Tina was waiting for her outside the door. They ran for the fire escape stairs. When they reached the lobby Sunshine grabbed her keys from Tina and began pushing the unlock on the keypad as they ran out of the hotel. She led Tina to her car, where they threw the bags in the back seat.

Tina crunk up the car and quickly pulled out of the parking lot with her heart racing like the winning horse of the Kentucky Derby. She drove in silence to the Motel 6 that was right around the corner from where they had just left. They checked into a room and Tina unloaded the drugs into the room while Sunshine hurried her naked body inside the room to take a shower.

When Sunshine got out of the shower and walked out the bathroom, Tina was sitting on the edge of the bed counting the kilos inside the duffle bags. Tina looked up from the duffle bags and saw Sunshine standing in front of her naked, drying off with a towel.

"Come here, baby, and let me thank you for the outstanding performance you did." Tina told her and Sunshine sat down on the bed beside her. Tina leaned over and kissed Sunshine on the lips.

Then she laid Sunshine onto her back. Tina rolled on top of Sunshine then leaned down and stuck her tongue inside her mouth. Sunshine loved Tina's aggressiveness. Even though she had always preferred men, Tina's touch had an electrifying sensation flowing through her body. Tina took her tongue out of Sunshine's mouth and kissed her neck down to her breast.

"Ahh Ahh" Sunshine gasped as she felt Tina begin to rub her inner thigh while she sucked on her dark brown nipples at the same time. Tina stopped sucking Sunshine's nipples and began kissing down past her navel to her soaking wet pussy. Tina peeled back Sunshine's pussy lips and licked her pink clitoris as she simultaneously stuck two fingers inside of Sunshine's sunny delight.

"Umm, ahh." Cried Sunshine as she felt something build up inside of her that she had never felt from anyone eating her pussy.

"You like that baby?" Tina drove her fingers deeper into Sunshine's pussy. Sunshine reached and grabbed a hold to Tina's head, feeling like she was about to explode.

"Baby, I'm finna cummmm," Said Sunshine through faint breathing. Tina then began sucking on her clit, sending Sunshine into an orgasm.

"Ooh shhit, ahhh baayy." Sunshine screamed as her body began jerking while she came in Tina's mouth. Pleased with her job, Tina crawled up to Sunshine's face and started kissing her passionately on the lips.

"No one has ever made me feel like that." Sunshine told Tina once their lips parted.

"That's just the beginning, baby. I got you. Let's get some rest." Tina told her and they cuddled under the bed sheets and went to sleep.

♦ ♦ ♦

Five minutes after Sunshine and Tina left the room, Eric noticed that he and Sammie were alone. He pushed Sammie from off top of him and jumped out of the couch bed. He ran through the room looking for the girls, but they were gone. Sammie finally realized what Eric already knew and he ran to the bathroom. When he saw the duffle bags were gone from the closet, he fell to his knees.

"Nooo!" Sammie screamed to the top of his lungs. He knew that he had fucked up in a major way. Not only did he get robbed, he got robbed for something that was worth three times the value of the product he was supposed to have. Sammie knew Mandy was gonna kill him if he didn't get the dope back from Tina and Sunshine.

Eric threw on his clothes and went into the bathroom where Sammie was at on the floor butt naked, crying like a bitch. What the fuck is he; crying for, thought Eric when he saw the open briefcase with stacks of money inside of it, plus a kilo on the floor and the kilo on the sink.

"Aye man, give me my money so I can get up out this bitch." Eric was ready to go.

"Fuck you. Those bitches stole fifty kilos from me. I'm gonna kill those bitches." What the fuck, thought Eric, not believing what he had just heard Sammie say. Sammie stood up and handed Eric $20,000.

"I need you to help me find those bitches. I will give you more money and a kilo of cocaine."

"Okay, cool." Eric stuffed the money into his pockets.

Eric tried to call Sunshine while Sammie got dressed, but her phone kept going to the voicemail. After Sammie got dressed he called Nathan and informed on what happened. Next he called Vanilla but he didn't get an answer. Minutes later Sammie, Eric and Nathan piled into Sammie's new Range Rover and went hunting for the girls.

Chapter Twenty-Nine

So the pregnancy symptoms were real, thought Greg as he turned into Accent Creek Apartments located on the east side of Nashville. He was glad that he had met Delhia because if he didn't, he probably would've never known his son existed. Even though Greg would've loved to been laying in the bed more than likely running dick in and out of Delhia, he had some business to handle while the opportunity presented itself at the very moment. Greg was about to move forward with his life and he didn't want any superfluous bullshit going on in his life. He grabbed his 4-4 bulldog from the passenger seat as he parked in front of the building he was looking for. Greg stepped out of his car and stuck his gun in his waist line. Then he pulled his wallet from his back pocket and took out the key that he had paid the maintenance man three grand for. Greg walked up the steps to the apartment door and looked at his watch which read 4:13 a.m. Comfortable in his mind that the people inside were asleep, Greg pulled his gun from his waist then he unlocked the door. He stepped inside the apartment to find there wasn't anybody in the front room. Nasty Bitch pussy ain't healed up yet and she already fuckin, thought Greg as he scanned the room and noticed the man of the house's gun was laying on the table.

Greg walked towards the back to the bedroom. The bedroom door was wide open allowing Greg to see and hear the two individuals in bed sleeping. Greg stepped into the bedroom and flicked on the light switch, but neither of the people woke up. Oh how cute, thought Greg as he looked at Miquel and Nicole sleeping. Greg walked to the foot of the bed and picked it up a few inches with his free hand then dropped it, causing Miquel and Nicole to wake up. They rose from their sleep to find Greg standing at the foot of the bed with a big revolver pointed in their direction. They were both petrified by the sight of Greg, who was slightly smiling, which was extra scary.

"Good morning to you, you sons ah bitches. This shit is gonna be real quick and to the point." Greg had their undivided attention as he waved his pistol back and forth between the two of them.

"First things first. If ern one of you say a mumbling muthafuckin word, I'm gonna shoot you in your fuckin face." Greg paused as he stared into the eyes of two people that at one point in time in his life, he had love for, in one way or the other.

Seeing that Miquel wasn't bout that gangsta shit for real and Nicole was scared to death, Greg decided to carry on.

"I've been knowing about ya'll's affair for some time now, but I was too busy building my empire, plus I thought you were pregnant by me but DNA proved differently. I'm not mad at either of you because I respect the game, but ya'll will stay the fuck out of my lane."

Greg stopped talking and he pulled the hammer back on the revolver he had in his hand. Miquel tensed up, not knowing what Greg's next move was going to be and Nicole started praying to God while she stared at the man she had fucked over.

"I don't want anything from the house nor do I want anything to do with you. If either one of you come near me or anything I'm associated with, I will personally kill you. Miquel, your beef with Delhia is over, unless you wanna die right now. Is there a problem? Greg taunted Miquel with his gun. Miquel shook his head no, remembering that Greg said he didn't want to hear a mumbling word.

"Good! Now ya'll have a nice life together." Greg left out of the bedroom and then left Miquel's apartment.

Nicole jumped into Miquel's arms while he sat in the bed speechless and dismayed from Greg's surprise appearance. Miquel knew that Greg meant every word he said, but he couldn't let Nicole think he was some type of ho ass nigga that was gonna let a nigga come into his house and punk him. Miquel moved Nicole to the side, jumped out of the bed and ran to the front room. He grabbed his 9mm from off the table and went to the front door, which Greg left open when he left. Miquel saw a customized Ferrari leaving the apartment complex and he knew it was Greg. Damn that bitch nigga flexin, thought Miquel as he closed and locked his front door.

He knew he had to move right away. Ain't no way in the hell I can stay here and how that nigga know about Delhia? Miquel asked himself as he sat on his couch lost in his thoughts with his nerves badder than ah muthafucka.

◆ ◆ ◆

"Big bruh, I'm telling you that shit is fire enough to cut at least four times." Trap explained to Mandy as they pulled into the garage of the stash house in Mandy's candy red Ferrari 458, sitting on offset Forgiato wheels.

"Oh yeah! Well, ill bruh, I got fifty more in here for you, but after I get rid of everything I think I'm gonna give the game up." Mandy told Trap as they walked into the stash house.

Trap was Mandy's right hand man. He knew everything that went on in the hoods of Nashville and he was an extreme hustla. Trap was eighteen years old, standing 5'9 ", weighing 190 and he had the heart of a lion. He met Mandy four years ago at a neighborhood gas station.

On that day, Mandy pulled into the gas station and parked his liquorish black 69 Cutlass at the pump. Trap was sitting on a milk crate when he saw Mandy's car pull up. He didn't care about how fancy the car was. The only thing he cared about was getting the person who was driving the car to let him pump their gas for them in exchange for some currency. Pumping gas had been Trap's hustle for the past two months. It was how he fed himself and his lil brother, Teddy, since they ran away from foster care. Trap and Teddy had been placed in foster care after their mom overdosed on heroin and they didn't have any family members willing to take them in. The day the people at the foster care tried to split them up, they ran away from the facility. Trap would pay a crackhead to stay at their house every night with what he hustled up on at the store so he and his brother would have somewhere to lay their heads at night.

When Mandy pulled up at the store Trap jumped up from the crate he was sitting on and ran to the driver window of the car. Mandy saw a lil dusty nigga with the look of hunger in his eyes, standing outside his car so he rolled the window down. As soon as the window came down, Trap asked if he could pump Mandy's gas or make a store run for him. Mandy decided to see what type of head the lil nigga had on his shoulders. Mandy gave him a hundred dollar bill, and told him to bring him a box of cigarillos, two Red Bulls, a box of Magnums, a box of Newport shorts, a lighter, two dollars worth of gizzards with hot sauce, and a blue Icee. Trap went into the store and returned to Mandy's car in five minutes with Mandy's exact order.

Mandy knew Trap wasn't the average dumb ass lil nigga hangin at the store so he told Trap to ride with him. Trap told him the only way he would go is if his lil brother could come and Mandy agreed. Mandy took them shopping and out to eat at Joe's Crab Shack. While they ate, Trap filled Mandy in on him and his brother's situation. He told Mandy he needed a job to support him and Teddy.

Mandy saw loyalty in Trap's eyes and decided to take him under his wing. From that day forth Mandy started installing everything about the dope game and life into Trap.

"Hell yeah, Big Bruh gone let me run this checkup before you say good-bye to the game." Said Trap as he took a seat at the bar while Mandy walked to the back room.

When Mandy walked into the back room, he immediately got mad when he saw that the duffle bags on the floor had white stickers on their straps. Sammie had gotten the wrong bags. The duffle bags with red stickers on the straps had heroin inside of them. Stupid bitch, thought Mandy as he walked back to the front where Trap was at. He pulled out his phone and called Sammie. Trap saw that Mandy's jawline kept tightening so he knew that Mandy was mad about something. It was a characteristic Trap learned about Mandy a few months after they met. Mandy dialed Sammie's number again, put his phone on speaker phone and laid it on the bar. He listened to the phone ring while he got a Corona out of the refrigerator and began to drink it.

When Sammie's voicemail came on, Mandy kept his cool and ended the call. He sat his beer down and rested his elbows on the bar. He began massaging his temple with his, thumbs as he thought of why Sammie wasn't answering the phone. And why the fuck did he take my heroin, thought Mandy.

"Damn, son son, old Sammie done fucked up again I believe." Mandy stood up from the bar and killed his beer.

"What it do, Big Bruh?" Trap asked Mandy, seeing that Mandy had some heavy shit on his mind.

"Ion know yet, but shit will hit the fan today I betcha, but fuck it. Let's go to the mall to see if we can get Teddy those J's that came out this morning." Mandy grabbed the keys to his black on black Range Rover and he and Trap left the stash house.

◆ ◆ ◆

Sammie laid across the bed naked and bug eyed as he looked at Mandy's name appear on the screen of his phone. When he, Eric and Nathan made it back from searching for the girls, Sammie told Nathan to leave him and Eric alone. As soon as Nathan left the room, Sammie and Eric got high and got their freak on. Sammie figured he might as well enjoy himself while he still had breath in his body.

Eric had sold his soul to the devil for a small price and he didn't even know it. After he and Sammie had sex, Sammie showered Eric with more money and gave him a key of cocaine. Eric told Sammie he would stay with him until they found the girls and got the dope back.

"Who's that calling?" Eric asked Sammie when he noticed how timorous Sammie started acting as he looked at his phone while it rang.

"Oh, um, that's just my nephew. I'll call him back," Sammie tried to downplay the situation, but his fidgeting let Eric know that it might be trouble calling his phone. Sammie knew his time was running out. He was so high, he couldn't think straight. All he could do was wish he woke up from the nightmare he was living.

◆ ◆ ◆

Chapter Thirty

It was 10 a.m. when Chocolate was awakened from her sleep by the smell of pancakes, cheese eggs and bacon. She rolled over and looked at Vanilla, who was snoring like a hog. Chocolate got out of the bed, went to the bathroom, brushed her teeth and washed her face. She was glad she had bought her mother the house that they stayed in. She bought it for her mom six months ago when she counted her first hundred thousand dollars. It only seemed right in Chocolate's eye for her to buy her mother a house before she bought herself something she wanted. Leslie had always put Chocolate before herself. Chocolate was her only baby. Leslie was hurt when Chocolate dropped out of college and started living the wild life, but Chocolate was her baby so she loved her unconditionally no matter what she did. After she brushed her pearly whites, Chocolate walked into the kitchen to find her mother standing over the stove whipping and flipping.

"Mauh, that smell good or I'm just super hungry." Said Chocolate as she sat down at the island bar in the kitchen and opened her Facebook up on her iPhone.

"Child you just hungry." Said Leslie as she cut off the eyes on the stove.

Chocolate scrolled through her Facebook page, noticing all the post people had posted were mainly pertaining to how Club OG's was off the chain the night before. She continued browsing, looking at the pictures some of the people she knew had taken at the club. Chocolate saw a live streaming video that was uploaded by Dream Catcher, one of the popular strippers in the South region.

Chocolate sipped on her orange juice as she clicked on the video and waited for it to start playing. When the video started playing Chocolate damn near choked, causing orange juice to fly from her mouth when she saw Delhia behind Dream Catcher throwing major money with some fine ass nigga behind her, draped in diamonds.

"Cidney is your ass all right?" Leslie asked Chocolate while she fixed her plate.

"No, Mauh. This is the woman Tina has been in love with for the past year, in this video at the club with some man. He fine too, Mama, come look." Chocolate told Leslie who had just finished fixing Chocolate's plate. Leslie walked over to Chocolate carrying her food. Chocolate stood up to show her mother the video.

"Girl, what man are you talking about?" Said Leslie. "Right there, mama. Behind the woman throwing the money."

Leslie focused her eyes on the sexy black specimen.

"Oh my God! " Leslie then accidentally dropped the plate of food she was holding. She took the phone from Chocolate and started the video over. Leslie had to sit down.

"Mama Look what you done! What's wrong with you?" Chocolate asked her mama seeing that she had to take a seat and she wasn't studying the food she had dropped. Leslie sat in silence for a moment.

"That's Greg, Cidney, your father." Chocolate then bent down to get a closer look at the man.

"Mama, how are you sure?" Chocolate asked Leslie as they watched the video again.

"The way that man fucked me, I could never forget his face." Leslie said with a Kool-Aid smile.

"Eww, Mauh. I don't want to hear all that." Chocolate playfully pushed Leslie in the shoulder.

"I'm just keeping it real, but don't you know the woman he with because if you do, you need to call her so we can get in touch with ya daddy." Leslie told Chocolate, who quickly logged out from Facebook and went to her contacts in her iPhone to call Delhia.

This shit is crazy, thought Chocolate as she called Delhia's phone.
RING   RING   RING

Delhia was sitting on the edge of the bed next to Greg's feet, feeding CJ when her phone started ringing. She reached behind herself and picked up the phone. I wonder what she want, thought Delhia when she saw Chocolate's number.

"Hello, Black girl!" answered Delhia.

"Hey Del Del. What you doing?" Asked Chocolate. "Nothing. Feeding my baby! What's up?"

"I need a favor from you." "Okay. What's up?"

"The man you were with last night in the club. I really need to get in touch with him. Chocolate sounded sincere.

"If it's really important, I can wake him up. But if it's not, I'd rather you call back later."

"I promise you it's very important." Chocolate smiled at Leslie, who was eavesdropping.

"Okay baby. Hold on." Delhia started shaking Greg's leg. "Bay, get up. Somebody needs to talk to you." Greg turned over and reached for the phone with his eyes still closed. Delhia put the phone in his hand.

"Yeah!" Grumbled Greg. Chocolate wanted to just hang up the phone, but she felt that her mother knew what she was talking about.

"Hi. This is Cidney Preston, Leslie's daughter." Chocolate watched her mother smile from ear to ear. Delhia's phone volume was on high, so Delhia could hear Chocolate. Greg immediately opened his eyes and rose up, sitting erect in the bed.

"I love you! Baby I'm so sorry!" said Greg. Delhia looked at him like he was crazy. Chocolate was astounded by his response. "Are you....." Chocolate started to say before she was cut off.

"Yes baby, I'm your father." Greg said, cutting Chocolate off.

Chocolate was lost for words. She felt her emotions build up inside of her and a tear ran down her cheek.

"Baby girl, are you there?"

"Yes. I'm here" replied Chocolate and Greg heard the cracking in her voice. Then she started sniffing. Delhia knew what was going on and she motioned for Greg to give her the phone.

"Black girl, can you come to my house right now?" Delhia asked Chocolate who had started crying uncontrollably in the phone. Leslie took the phone from Chocolate.

"Hi! This is Cidney's mother, Leslie. I'm gonna bring her over there right now. She's just a little emotional, but we're on the way." Leslie explained while Chocolate cried on her shoulder.

"Okay. We're waiting on ya'll. She knows the address." Said Delhia as she watched Greg climb out of the bed.

"Okay, hun. We'll see you in a minute." Leslie hung up the phone and held Chocolate in her arms.

"Come on, baby. It's gonna be okay. Let's go meet your father." Leslie said as she let go of Chocolate, who was gaining control of her emotional roller coaster.

◆ ◆ ◆

Greg walked around the bed to Delhia and took CJ out of her arms.

"Ughh, he needs to be burped!" Delhia protested, but she quickly got side tracked when she saw Greg's dick hanging from the bottom of his boxers.

Greg started patting CJ softly on his back so he would burp. Delhia was getting on some other shit as she examined Greg's chiseled physique. Her pussy got wet and her hand reached for the prize in her eyes. Greg suddenly felt Delhia grab his manhood and began stroking it with her soft hands.

"Girl, you better stop!" Greg didn't mean a single word.

Delhia paid his words no attention and she put the head of his dick into her mouth.

"Ah, shit bay." said Greg as he felt Delhia's warm mouth cover the head of his dick. Then Delhia released from her mouth and hands.

"You're right. I need to stop. Let me get ready for our company." Delhia stood up smiling seductively a t Greg then she walked to the bathroom.

"You's a dirty muthafucka. I got you bay! I promise you that." Greg yelled between his laughs.

Man, God is good! I get to meet both of my kids in twenty four hours. I gotta call Meko, thought Greg as he sat CJ down on the bed and got his phone. Delhia walked inside the bathroom then closed and locked the door. She reached inside the shower and turned it on. When she turned her head she was startled when she looked through the blinds of her bathroom window which was the size of a door and saw Brian in the backyard working. Delhia didn't know what it was about the young man, but every time she saw him her body demanded for her to touch herself. She tried to fight the temptation of the thoughts running through her mind, but she lost the battle against the tingling sensation that was present in her love box. She pulled the draw string to the blinds on the window to get Brian's attention.

KNOCK   KNOCK

After the second knock, Brian raised his head and saw Delhia who was about twenty five feet away from him, standing in the window of her bathroom. Delhia flashed a big smile and waved at Brian. He smiled and waved back. Delhia immediately began peeling her clothes off since she had his attention. When she was fully naked, Delhia cocked her right foot up on the side of the tub and began rubbing on her bald pussy. Delhia rubbed in circular motion on her clitoris while her eyes were focused on Brian who started groping on his dick through his jeans.

"She got your daddy fucked up if she think she ain't about to let me slide up in those guts." Greg told CJ right after he hung the phone up from talking to Meko.

Greg heard when Delhia locked the door when she went into the bathroom and he had already came up with a plan to get inside. He got a clothes hanger out of her closet, stretched the top of it and stuck it into the hole of the door knob. Click! Bingo, thought Greg when he picked the lock. He then began slowly turning the knob and he eased the door barely open.

Once the door was open enough, Greg stuck his in for a peep.

"What the fuck?" Greg said to himself as his eyes widened and wrinkles spread across his forehead from seeing Delhia with her foot cocked up on the side of the tub while she penetrated her pussy with two fingers.

To put the fork in the steak, Greg could see Brian in the backyard with his pants down, jacking his dick while he watched Delhia fuck herself. And I thought I was ah prison nigga, thought Greg as he heard what sounded like Delhia was about to climax.

"Ahh, ahh, umm," moaned Delhia as she reached her peak.

Greg took the opportunity to close the door and then he went and sat on the bed next to CJ. I can't fuck with this bitch, she throwed like a frisbee, thought Greg as he picked up CJ and played with him till minutes later when he heard the shower cut off. When Delhia walked out of the bathroom Greg picked up his phone and called Big Hurt.

"What's up, Boss?" said Hurt.

"It's your world, baby boy. Meet me at the spot. I'm on my way there now." Greg looked at Delhia who was standing in front of him with a towel wrapped around her.

"I'm on my way boss." "Bet." Greg hung up.

"You know that girl on her way over here!" said Delhia. "Yeah, give me her number." Delhia got her phone off the dresser and gave Greg Chocolate's number. Greg called Chocolate. "Hello." answered Chocolate.

"Baby Girl, you know where Club OG's is at, don't you?" "Yeah, we about eight minutes from there."

"Go there! I'll be there in ten minutes." Greg hung up the phone and quickly threw on his clothes.

He kissed CJ and stood up and left without saying anything to Delhia. Delhia felt as if Greg was acting funny as she watched him walk out the front door to get in his car. It wasn't until she walked back to her room, set on the bed and began lotioning her legs, when she saw the clothes hanger on the floor with the top of it stretched out. You stupid bitch, thought Delhia as she stared at the hanger knowing that Greg had picked the lock and saw her playing in her. pussy. Delhia rested her elbows on her thighs and buried her face into her hands while she shook her head in disbelief of her actions.

Ten minutes after Greg left the house, Delhia's doorbell rang. She figured it was Greg since he had left his wallet and Rolex on the dresser.

She tied up her robe, slid her feet into her house shoes and went to the front door.

"I figured you….." Delhia started saying as she opened the door, but she quickly shut up when she saw Brian standing in front of her.

"Hi, Beautiful." Brian said, smiling.

"Hi. Can I help you?" said Delhia treating him like a total stranger as if she just didn't masturbate with him minutes ago.

"Could I please have a few bottles of water?" Brian asked nicely, looking like he was very thirsty.

"Sure. Come in while I grab them out of the fridge." Brian stepped in the house and closed the door.

"I'm sorry to bother you." Brian apologized.

"No, you're fine! I want to apologize for my behavior earlier though, I don't want you to think I'm some old freak." Delhia explained while she walked to the refrigerator.

She thought Brian was gonna respond to her remark but he didn't. When Delhia came out of the refrigerator with the two bottles of water, Brian wrapped his powerful hands around Delhia's throat and choke slammed her, hitting her head on the marble counter, knocking her unconscious……

To be continued.